"What has long been a taboo topic between employer and employee, and an often angst ridden journey for expectant mothers and employers alike, now for the first time has a playbook. Not only that, it hits on every note. You need not look any further for how to handle a maternity leave, and run your human capital, with the best information out there. This is progress."

Carolyn Lawrence, *Leader, Gender Diversity and Inclusion, Deloitte Canada*

"After reading through the Canadian Women's Maternity Leave Career Transitions guidebook, I wish I could have read this before I went through my own maternity leaves a few years ago. It's a well-researched, well written guide not only for employers to consider but also for women taking maternity leave. This is an excellent resource for any leave, not just maternity leave. The helpful check-lists and definitions are going to provide much needed support for any organization hoping to do better in how maternity leaves, or any leave, is managed."

Michelle Beck, *VP People & Culture, ATB Financial*

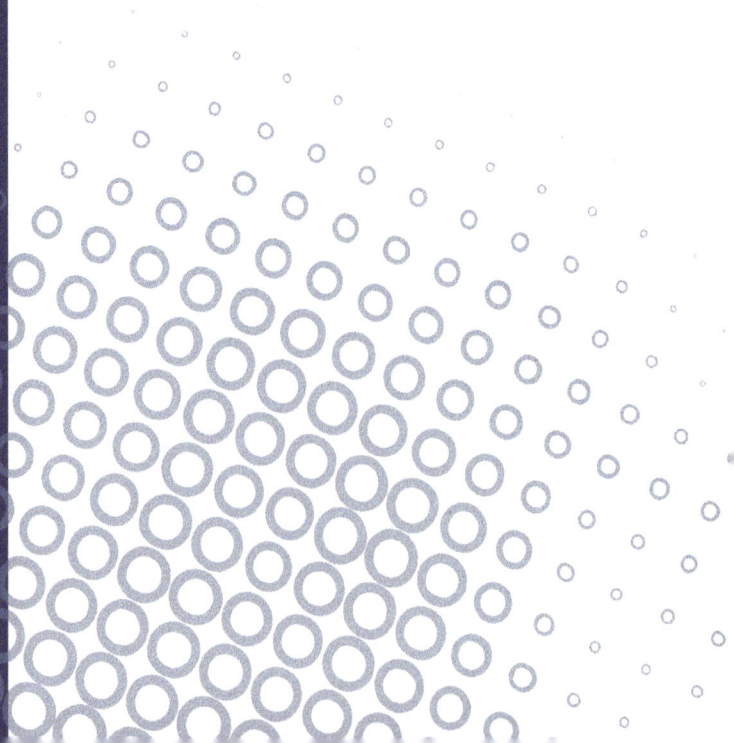

Making It Work!

How to effectively manage maternity leave career transitions

— AN EMPLOYER'S GUIDE —

Avra Davidoff, Laura Hambley, April Dyrda, Julie Choi,
Colleen Lucas, Rebecca Teebay-Webb

ceric
CANADIAN EDUCATION AND RESEARCH INSTITUTE FOR COUNSELLING
INSTITUT CANADIEN D'ÉDUCATION ET DE RECHERCHE EN ORIENTATION

Canada Career Counselling
Connecting the pieces

Making it Work!
Copyright 2016 by Avra Davidoff, Laura Hambley, April
Dyrda, Julie Choi, Colleen Lucas, Rebecca Teebay-Webb

Editor: Sheryl Khanna

Wholesale discounts for book orders are
available through Ingram Distributors.

Tellwell Talent
www.tellwell.ca

Published by:
Canadian Education and Research Institute for Counselling
(CERIC)
2 St Clair Avenue East, Suite 300
Toronto, Ontario
M4T 2T5
Canada
website: www.ceric.ca
Email: admin@ceric.ca

ISBN
Paperback: 978-1-988066-05-9
EBook: 978-1-988066-06-6

Contents

Acknowledgments

This project was funded by the Canadian Education and Research Institute of Counselling (CERIC), who we thank for enthusiastically recognizing the need for this project. We would also like to thank the research and content development team at Canada Career Counselling, whose career and life experiences, as well as passion for career development, are infectious and inspiring. In addition, we would also like to thank the many employees and employers from across Canada, who provided valuable insights and feedback through focus groups, surveys, and interviews. And finally, to all of our community partners and organizations who supported and promoted this project from development to dissemination, we thank you for helping to make a difference for mothers in Canada and the organizations who employ them.

Project Team

Avra Davidoff - Project Lead, Researcher, Content Developer

Avra Davidoff is a workplace psychologist and Associate at Canada Career Counselling and the Leadership Success Group. She currently practices in the areas of career development, leadership development, and diversity. Avra holds a Master's in Counselling Psychology, with a career counselling specialization, from the Graduate Centre for Applied Psychology at Athabasca University.

Dr. Laura Hambley – Project Advisor, Researcher, Content Developer

Dr. Laura Hambley founded Canada Career Counselling and has worked in the field of career development since 2001. Laura holds a Master's in Applied Psychology and a PhD in Industrial/Organizational Psychology from the University of Calgary. As an Adjunct Professor of Psychology, Laura regularly contributes to research in career development.

April Dyrda - Research Assistant, Content Developer

April Dyrda is pursuing her Master's in Counselling Psychology at the University of Calgary. She currently works as a practicum counsellor at Mount Royal University and serves as a student mentor through the Canadian Psychological Association and the University of Calgary. Her research is based on the career development of post-secondary students.

Julie Choi - Research Assistant, Content Developer

Julie Choi is an Industrial/Organizational Psychology Consultant with a broad range of skills. Julie received her MSc in Industrial/Organizational Psychology from the University of Calgary in 2014, and is currently completing her PhD with a focus on understanding the factors that influence how a subordinate views their leader.

Dr. Colleen Lucas – Researcher, Content Developer

Dr. Colleen Lucas holds a PhD in Industrial/Organizational Psychology from the University of Calgary. She lives in Calgary and practices in the areas of career counselling, and leadership assessment and development. Her research interests include psychological contract violation in the workplace, organizational learning and change, and career and leadership development.

Rebecca Teebay-Webb - Researcher, Content Developer

Rebecca Teebay-Webb is a Registered Provisional Psychologist with the College of Alberta Psychologists. She practices in the areas of career, personal and trauma counselling, and works with both adults and adolescents. Rebecca holds a Master's in Counselling Psychology from Yorkville University, and a BSc from the University of Liverpool.

Dr. Stephanie Paquet – Researcher

Dr. Stephanie Paquet is a Senior Associate Consultant with Knightsbridge Leadership Solutions in Calgary. She has consulted with organizations in a variety of industries in the area of talent management, including the design of selection systems, facilitation of leadership development initiatives, succession planning, leadership coaching, 360 feedback, and psychological and behavioural assessments for selection and development. Stephanie is a graduate of McGill University and holds an MSc and PhD in Industrial/Organizational Psychology from the University of Calgary.

Genevieve Hoffart - Research Assistant

Genevieve Hoffart is an MSc candidate in Industrial/Organizational Psychology at the University of Calgary, and research coordinator in the Individual and Team Performance Lab, where she manages key research partnerships. She is passionate about developing applicable tools and workshops to improve the functioning of teams in organizations across North America.

Travis Schneider - Research Assistant

Travis Schneider is an Industrial/Organizational Psychology Consultant who leverages his expertise in assessment to guide clients on their career paths. Travis holds an MSc in Industrial/Organizational Psychology from the University of Western Ontario, and is currently completing his PhD on the validity of social media for job selection.

Dr. Roberta Neault - Reviewer

Dr. Roberta Neault is an award-winning leader in career development, in Canada and internationally. Roberta is the President of Life Strategies Ltd., as well as the Associate Dean of the Faculty of Behavioural Sciences at Yorkville University. In both roles Roberta manages predominantly female faculty, staff, and students, where navigating maternity leaves is an ongoing reality.

Kathleen Johnston - Reviewer

Kathleen Johnston is a Career Strategist who is passionate about facilitating women to live and work in their "unique zone of genius." She is a counselling therapist, executive coach, stress consultant, career development instructor for over ten years, and contributing writer for the first Canadian colleges/universities career text. Kathleen holds a BSc in Family Studies from the University of Alberta and MA in Pastoral Psychology and Counselling from St. Stephen's College.

Funding

The funding for this project was provided by the Canadian Education and Research Institute for Counselling (CERIC). CERIC is a charitable organization that advances education and research in career counselling and career development, in order to increase the economic and social well-being of Canadians.

Introduction

Welcome to *Making It Work! How to Effectively Manage Maternity Leave Career Transitions: An Employer's Guide.* This resource was developed for anyone who employs, leads, manages, trains, coaches, or otherwise supports pregnant, adoptive, and parenting women in the workplace; including, but not limited to, Human Resource (HR) professionals and practitioners, managers and leaders, business owners, consultants, coaches, and career development practitioners. By taking the time to review this resource, you are investing not only in your **employees**, but in your organization and in yourself.

Whether you have been supporting women on maternity leave for years or you are doing so for the first time, this guidebook is a comprehensive manual that accommodates the diverse needs of all employers. All types of workplaces can benefit from learning about proven practices, and how to implement these practices in their organizations. However, depending on the type and size of organization you represent, the programs and offerings you can provide to women will vary. By sharing a variety of stories from past trials and successes, and presenting promising, yet modifiable leading practices, we hope to ensure the best possible outcomes for all mothers, employers, and the communities in which organizations and employees both function. In effect, most of the content we suggest in this guidebook is applicable to workplaces which are small and large, local and global, urban and rural, across all sectors (private, public, nonprofit), unionized and non-unionized, privately held and publically traded, and new businesses and start-ups, as well as organizations that have been around for many generations. This guidebook is also equally applicable to women who are experiencing their first or subsequent maternity leave career transition; as each transition offers its own unique challenges and opportunities.

Certainly not exhaustive in its scope, this resource is meant to be a self-directed tool that you can use to tailor specific strategies to the needs of your organization and employees. As an **employer**, it can be difficult to set aside sufficient time, or find relevant information, to assist employees with maternity leave career transitions, other than information which is typically obtained through an organization's policies and procedures. However, these resources are often guided by legislation and while useful, this information does not provide organizations with information to help guide their employee's development.

Our goal is to provide you with both convenient and user-friendly information, which will equip you to adopt a proactive and positive approach in managing maternity leave career transitions. By taking the initiative to effectively manage these transitions, you are setting yourself and your employees up for success. And, as Benjamin Franklin so poignantly noted, "By failing to prepare, you are preparing to fail."

Although we use the term employer throughout this resource, the term is meant to be inclusive of all managers, supervisors, business owners, and inclusive of workplaces of all sizes, types, and structures.

We have defined some additional key terms used in this guidebook to ensure a common understanding for our readers. The key terms are included in bold the first time they appear and are defined in the Glossary at the end of the guidebook. We hope that by using this resource you are informed and inspired to *Make It Work!*

PURPOSE AND POTENTIAL

While there are a variety of maternity leave resources available, most focus on legal, or health-related topics, such as employment insurance, employment law, **postpartum depression**, breastfeeding or **work-life integration**. There is very limited information that Canadian employers can use to understand the career transition associated with maternity leave and the experiences of new and **expectant mothers** (mothers who, through birth or adoption, are expecting the arrival of a child). We recognize that not all organizations are the same, nor are all organizations privileged with the finances and resources to implement comprehensive career development programs for transitioning employees. The information contained in this guidebook and the employee version (*Making It Work: How to Effectively Navigate Maternity Leave Career Transitions: An Employee's Guide*) is meant to serve as a starting point for your organization to determine leading practices for effectively managing **maternity leave career transitions**, which are changes in the new/expectant mother's employment as a result of pregnancy, birth, or adoption.

On a broader scale, our goal is that this guidebook, along with the employee version (*Making It Work! How to Effectively Navigate Maternity Leave Career Transitions: An Employee's Guide*) will allow you to understand and address existing or potential obstacles that prevent your organization and working mothers from realizing their potential. In turn, this resource provides you with an opportunity to stimulate discussion and collaboration to determine leading and promising practices for handling maternity leave transitions, and women's career development as a whole. This discussion can occur both within and between organizations, industries, and professionals. Through discussion and collaboration, you can establish benchmarks, build capacities, and develop competencies in your organization. By taking a proactive approach to creating an **inclusive workplace** culture for *all* working mothers, you can transfer these experiences and learnings to facilitate an inclusive culture for all of your employees. And while there is much pressure on employers to act in socially responsible ways and to do the right thing, we sometimes overlook the evidence, which suggests that doing the *right* thing can also be the *strategic* thing to do.

Making It Work!
A CANADIAN PERSPECTIVE

Between the fall of 2013 and the spring of 2015, Canada Career Counselling embarked on a mission to understand the perceptions of both employees and employers regarding the impact of maternity leave on a woman's career development. Our research team conducted focus groups, one-on-one interviews, and a national survey, which culminated in the creation of this resource, webinars for both employers and employees, and articles in various publications. Webinars will be made available through Canada Career Counselling's Website (www.canadacareercounselling.com), as well as through CERIC's Website (www.ceric.ca).

DEMOGRAPHICS

Two focus groups were conducted with ten employers working in the province of Alberta who had personal experience with their staff taking maternity leave(s). Key themes and findings from these sessions were used to guide interview and survey questions. One-on-one interviews were held with fourteen employers from across Canada working in the nonprofit (29%), public (21%), and private (50%) sectors. A total of seventy-three employers completed the survey portion of this research study (six males, sixty-seven females). Surveyed employers most commonly represented the private sector (45%), as well as the public sector (32%), followed by those in nonprofit (20%), and other industries (3%).

Percentage of Participants from Represented Industries

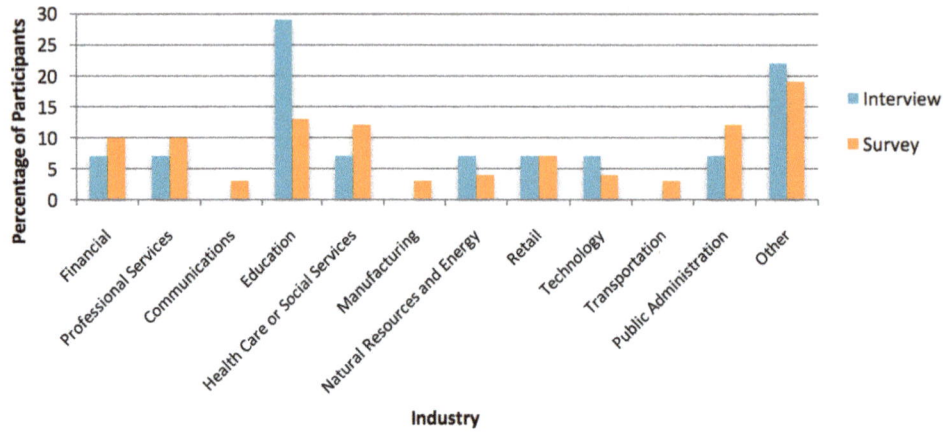

Participants included individuals across Canada from a wide array of positions, including HR specialists (31%), leaders (24%), managers and supervisors (24%), executives (6%), business owners (7%), and other employers (8%), such as consultants, directors, and advisors.

Percentage of Participants from Represented Provinces

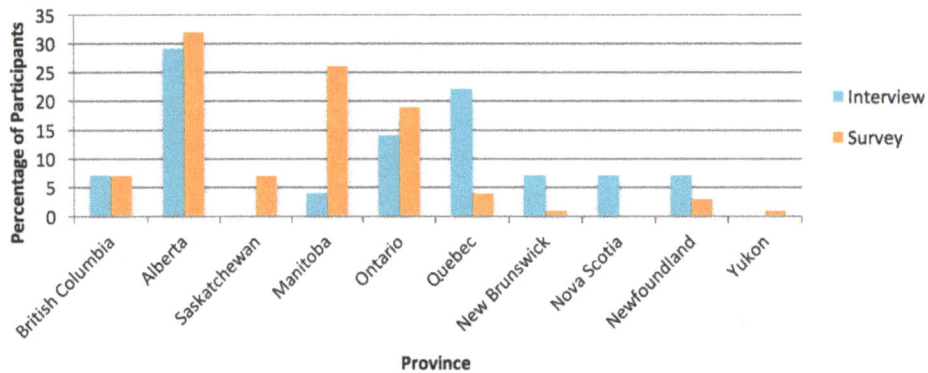

KEY THEMES

The vast majority of surveyed employers (85%) felt that maternity leave had either a neutral or positive impact on the career development of their employees. However, a disproportionately large number of new mothers (36%) felt that taking maternity leave had negatively impacted their opportunity for promotions, seniority, and career progression. Less than 4% of new mothers indicated that taking maternity leave had positively impacted their career.

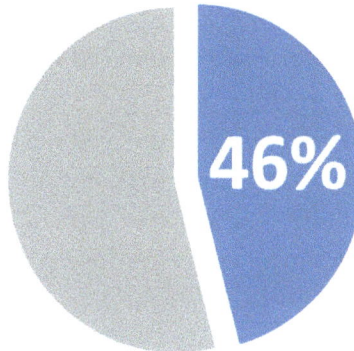

46% of employers felt that their organizations only **adequately** managed maternity leaves, with over half surveyed indicating that maternity leaves were managed **less than well.**

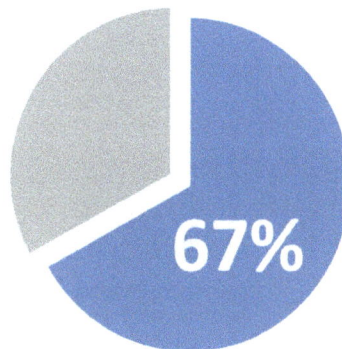

67% of employers indicated that they saw value in organizations taking action to better understand the maternity leave experience.

Employees on maternity leave come with their share of challenges and opportunities for both the individual and the organization. Below, you will find the three organizational benefits of maternity leave most commonly cited by employers.

1. **Developing a culture of support:** "If you can stick by your employees while they are away, they will stick by you when they return. You get a level of discretionary effort that you wouldn't have had otherwise." This quote from an employer we interviewed nicely summarizes a common theme that emerged in our research, which is that many employees returning from maternity leave will give back to the organization what they receive. When mothers are satisfied with the support from their organization, they are more likely to be not only committed to the organization, but also more productive in their role. Building a community and culture of support also fosters loyalty among other employees, increasing overall employee satisfaction.

Most Commonly Cited Organizational Benefits of Maternity Leave According to Employers

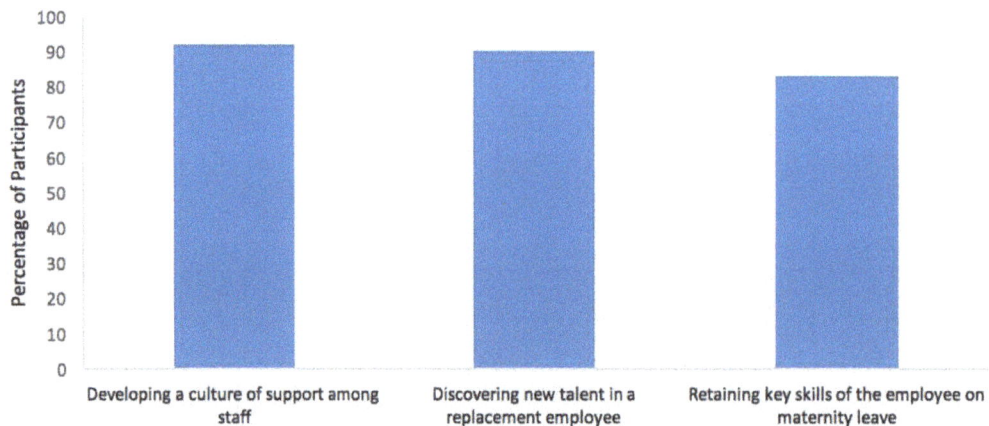

2. **Discovering new talent in a replacement employee:** Opening a position within an organization for someone to fill, either internally or externally, long-term or short-term, provides others with a developmental opportunity. For internal employees, this gives someone who is already a member of your team exposure to new areas of the organization.

When hiring from outside the organization, employers have the ability to find new talent that they would not have otherwise. In some cases, the employee who you hire to cover the maternity leave can be a good fit within the organization, and can be retained by the organization even after the maternity leave is over.

3. **Retaining key skills of the employee on maternity leave:** "As an employer, I seek [to keep] employees returning from maternity leaves because they are very dedicated and focused on the value of working and what it adds to their own life." This quote from an employer we interviewed echoes the notion that keeping employees with your organization after they have returned from maternity leave demonstrates a level of commitment that is likely to be reciprocated by the employee.

LOST OPPORTUNITY

One of the employers we interviewed noted, "There isn't a lot offered to employees or their employers to prepare them for the maternity leave." Employers that we interviewed consistently made mention of the fact that, in many cases, it is left up to the employee to find out how to manage her maternity leave, with the organization being unwilling or unable to offer support and guidance. Below are several of the most mentioned areas that employers saw as room for improvement in managing maternity leave transitions. These and other suggestions have been discussed in detail throughout the guidebook. It is our hope that while reading this guidebook, you will develop a clearer understanding about how to best manage the maternity leave process.

Before the Maternity Leave

1. **Conduct an exit interview:** Have a structured conversation with your employee prior to her maternity leave so that each of you can express any questions and/or possible concerns. Review each of your expectations, including how the organization can better support the new/expectant mother. Further, you can discuss whether she has all of the necessary resources to be successful in her position before leaving, and upon returning to work.

2. **Establish a communication plan:** In collaborating with your employee, determine whether, and how often, you will communicate with her while she is away on maternity leave. Set clear guidelines about what will be discussed, and when, and how communication will be maintained (e.g., telephone, e-mail, text, mail or in person).

3. **Set clear guidelines:** Ensure that HR representatives and managers establish a clear plan for the employee before and during her maternity leave, and after her return to work. This includes structuring a return to work plan and covering important topics such as the date of return, reintegration actions, roles and responsibilities, as well as her work schedule and career options upon returning.

During the Maternity Leave

1. **Maintain the communication plan:** Take the initiative to uphold the established communication plan. This may include keeping your employee up-to-date on changes within the organization, informing her of and including her in upcoming events or celebrations, making her aware of relevant training opportunities, or simply checking in to see how she is doing.

2. **Remember that a mother on leave is still an employee:** Recognize that mothers on maternity leave are still essential members of the organization, and that they are still part of the team. Depending on your predetermined communication plan, there are likely several ways to keep your employee informed and engaged.

After the Maternity Leave

1. **Conduct a return to work interview:** It is important to recognize that an employee who is coming back to work from maternity leave is likely returning to work under new circumstances. Having an open dialogue about changes

The Federal Court of Appeal rejected arguments from Canadian National Railway and Canada Border Services Agency. It set out the requirements for establishing a prima facie case of discrimination based on family status: (1) that the child is under the supervision of the complainant; (2) that the childcare obligation at issue engages the complainant's legal responsibility as a parent, as opposed to personal choice; (3) that the complainant has made reasonable efforts to meet her childcare obligations through alternative solutions; and (4) that the challenged workplace rule interferes in a manner that is more than trivial with the fulfillment of the childcare obligation.

The Federal Court of Appeal is clear that human rights protection does not extend to personal family choices, such as "participation of children in dance classes, sports events like hockey tournaments and other similar voluntary activities." However, for both Ms. Johnstone and Ms. Seeley, the Court found, this was not the issue. For both women, the issue was their ability to fulfill their basic obligation to ensure that, if they were at work, their children were adequately cared for.

Women in Canada owe a big debt to Fiona Ann Johnstone and Denise Seeley, to the Canadian Human Rights Commission, and to the lawyers who represented Johnstone and Seeley. This struggle was long and slow. It was a big victory for women in the workplace, precisely because, for women, the conflict between work requirements and childcare responsibilities is a key equality issue. Women have been, and continue to be, penalized because they are the primary caregivers for children and other family members. This was a real step forward.

in roles and responsibilities will allow both parties to communicate effectively and share aspirations and career plans.

2. **Implement a re-onboarding process:** Managers, coworkers, and/or clients may assume that because a new mother is a returning employee, that she will be able to pick up where she left off; however, employees need to be re-integrated into their work roles, and into the social environment of the office, which takes conscious thought and focused attention.

3. **Discuss flexible work arrangements:** These options afford new mothers the opportunity to effectively manage their work and family lives. One of the employees we interviewed noted, "Knowing that your employer values you enough to offer you that option makes you more likely to stay." As an employer, consider what flexible arrangements you might be able to offer and how these can benefit both your employee and your organization.

4. **Make use of mentors or a buddy system:** Pair those about to go on, or newly returned from, maternity leave with someone in a similar role who has already been through the maternity leave process. This person can offer advice and support and facilitate a smooth transition back to the workplace.

Mother in the Modern Workplace
THE BUSINESS CASE

Building an effective business case is an essential management tool that supports and assists key decision makers in an organization. The business case for supporting mothers in the workplace is an important one. Many employers who adequately support expectant and parenting mothers in the workplace do so because it is the right thing to do, but it is also the strategic thing to do and makes good business sense.

"There are still huge opportunities for employers to be more attractive to working mothers. Support is often found in pockets or subcultures of an organization, but the acceptance of having children as being a part of life needs to be more widespread." - Employer Quote

LABOUR MARKET

While economists have long suggested that Canada could experience serious labour shortages in the near future, the more serious peril to Canadian employers and the economy is a skills mismatch, whereby the skills and talents of the labour pool do not meet labour market demands.[1] Although a solution does not exist to address this problem, part of the answer resides in attracting and using Canada's existing labour market as effectively as possible, and this includes working mothers.

Leveraging the skills and talents of working mothers is important for a host of reasons. Women make up approximately 50% of Canada's labour force and account for 58% of post-secondary graduates.[2] Of the working women who do become mothers, 90% will take a maternity leave, with forty-four weeks being the average length of leave.[3]

The employment rate for working mothers has increased steadily over the last three decades, and 73% of mothers report working in either a part-time or full-time capacity.[4] When viewed as a whole, mothers (including biological, adoptive, and stepmothers) account for 9.8 million members of Canada's current 35.7 million member population.[5] Clearly, working mothers are a significant component of the labour force. By recognizing and leveraging the opportunities this group presents, employers retain talent, enhance productivity, and decrease turnover.

LEGISLATIVE CONSIDERATIONS

For employers, there is a delicate balance between ensuring workplace productivity and supporting employees in meeting their personal commitments. Recent court cases have drawn focus to this issue, highlighting the occurrence of family status discrimination. In two separate cases, working mothers raised concerns that their caregiving responsibilities were used by the employer to unjustly discriminate against them *(Canadian National Railway Co. v. Seeley, and Canada [Attorney General] v. Johnstone)*. In both cases, the working mother requested alternate scheduling to accommodate her role as a caregiver. In both instances, the employer denied the employee's request for accommodation, with one employee being offered reduced hours, which would subsequently impact her benefits, pension and possible promotions, and the other employee was terminated.

As an employer, it is important to gather enough information and explore the relevant organizational policies, and provincial and federal legislation, to deal with such situations effectively. For additional information, organizations should consider exploring the following resource: *A Guide to Balancing Work and Caregiving Obligations: Collaborative approaches for a supportive and well-performing workplace*, produced by the Canadian Human Rights Commission.[6]

CORPORATE AND ECONOMIC GAINS

In their *New York Times* Best Seller, *Womenomics*, Claire Shipman and Katty Kay suggest that having women in strategic positions within an organization can increase organizational profitability.[7] According to *Catalyst*, a leading North American nonprofit research and advocacy organization dedicated to the advancement of women in the workplace, there is merit in this assertion.[8]

Catalyst researchers compared the financial performance of organizations that had more women on their boards of directors to organizations with no or fewer women on their boards, and found that the former outperformed the latter in the following ways: [9]

· Return on equity by 53%

· Return on sales by 42%

· Return on invested capital by 66%

"Legislation [around maternity leave] is all about 'thou shall not,' but there should be supplementary material which encourages 'thou shall.' For example, thou shall stay in touch with the employer, or thou shall keep up to date on training." - Employer Quote

---

So, why does the strategic placement of women in the workforce influence the bottom line? When women are placed in strategic positions and enabled to work effectively at all levels of the organization, there is noted increase in organizational creativity and innovation, a greater challenge to groupthink, improved customer understanding, and enriched corporate social practices.[10] These factors also improve the organization's corporate reputation and employers who effectively support women in the workplace can quickly become employers of choice. Given this information, it is unsurprising that the trend of impact investing is also growing. Specifically, impact investing occurs when investors look to buy stocks and make purchases from organizations that demonstrate socially responsible practices, not just in producing goods and services, but in attracting and managing employees. In a report released in January 2015, the Responsible Investment Association identified one trillion dollars' worth of assets being managed under the umbrella of ethical investing, which was an increase of 68% from the previous two years and accounts for 31% of the Canadian investment industry.[11] Therefore, for publicly listed organizations, supporting women's careers and maternity leave career transitions are worth promoting to investors as "good companies" are often good investments.

Further, in her book, *Making Diversity Work*, Carr-Ruffino suggests that organizations that are inclusive are also:[12]

- More adept at gaining and maintaining market shares locally and globally, and as such, are more proficient in understanding a diverse consumer base.

- More skilled at attracting talent through an improved corporate reputation.

- Better able to demonstrate organizational flexibility.

- Less susceptible to **groupthink**, thereby solving problems more effectively and creatively.

- Rewarded for their efforts. When employers are proactive in supporting employees in the workplace, employees perceive that they are valued and cared for, which in turn improves morale and productivity, and reduces absenteeism. Improved employee integration reduces workplace conflicts, including bullying, grievances and lawsuits, decreases health and safety concerns, and fosters trust and loyalty among **stakeholders.**

The bottom line is that when organizations create inclusive environments for working mothers, and take proactive steps in managing maternity leave career transitions, organizations are able to cut costs and increase profits.

Modern Maternity Leave

CAREER DEVELOPMENT, PROGRESSION AND ADVANCEMENT DEFINED

It is important to have a clear definition of some of the key words being used in this guidebook so that you can move your organization and employees forward with a common understanding. The following key words are defined in the Glossary, but we wanted to go into greater detail here with a few career-related key words and examples.

Career is the sum of all the paid and unpaid roles a working mother has held in her lifetime, and **career development** is the ongoing acquisition or refinement of knowledge, skills, and abilities. **Career progression**, or career advancement, refers to the movement towards a particular career goal(s), the achievement of which may or may not include change in title, responsibility, status, pay, flexibility, influence, or other factors which are determined by the mother as important and worthy of pursuit. Note the implication of this definition, that progression and advancement are non-directional (title, pay, or responsibility may increase or decrease), developmental in nature, and individually defined.

For example, a consultant or entrepreneur may hold the same title for the majority of her career, but may advance her skill set, expertise, customer base, and revenues as her career progresses. A working mother may also have different definitions of progress and advancement to correspond to different career and life circumstances. We often accept traditional notions of career progression and advancement, such as vertical movement and increase in pay, but there is some risk in using a one-dimensional ruler to measure the multiple facets of an employee's career. There are countless examples of employers assuming their employee wants to move into a higher-level position, as upward movement is generally considered to be a natural progression by management. In the case of the employee, there are many factors at play, and positions with increased responsibility may impact work/life integration and family values, and as a result this can be demotivating to some employees. Assuming the employee wants to move up in the organization is risky for employee engagement, succession planning, and retention.

Given that organizations are much flatter, that people transition within and between industries at quicker rates than previous generations, and that we have observed an increase in entrepreneurial and contract workers, our understanding of progression and advancement must also shift in response to these trends. If not, we risk projecting our ideas of success onto others and disengaging them from the work they were hired to perform.

ONE SOLUTION - MOVING FROM THE LADDER TO THE LATTICE

Adopting a modern take on career progression is one step you can take as an employer to address the previously noted concerns. While many are familiar with the metaphor of the career ladder, it is an outdated concept, and one that is quickly being replaced with the career lattice. While the **career ladder** characterizes career progression as a vertical movement, the **career lattice** conceptualizes career progression in more than one direction and can include horizontal, vertical, downward, and diagonal movement. The career lattice is responsive to the individual's life circumstance (e.g., family or health status), external factors influencing career development (e.g., the economy or existing opportunities within the organization), and promotes the collaboration and customization of careers and the structure of work. The career lattice encourages the continued growth of the organization and the employee by creating a variety of, and valuing, *all* career paths.

Modern **maternity leave**, which is inclusive of maternity, parental, and adoption leave, as well as any leave required for extended care following the birth or adoption of a child, is often viewed as a year off. As women begin their transition to maternity leave, it is not uncommon to hear the phrase, "Enjoy your year off!" Although well intentioned, this comment can cause mixed emotions (e.g., frustration, confusion, relief) among the transitioning mother as the phrase implies a vacation. Parents will tell you that although they recognize the opportunity and privilege of taking time away from a paid role to raise an infant, it is far from a vacation and is indeed one of the most difficult jobs. Organizations that convey maternity leave as a year off could negatively impact other aspects of a working mother's career, such as years of service, pensions, benefits, or salary, and could subsequently influence earning potential, developmental, and/or promotional opportunities, to name a few.

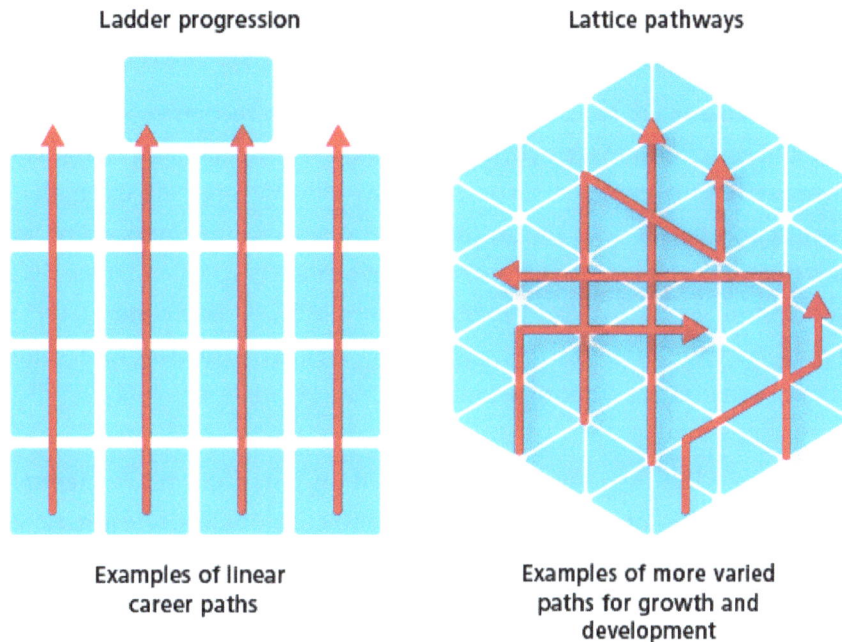

Ladder progression

Lattice pathways

Examples of linear
career paths

Examples of more varied
paths for growth and
development

Comparison of ladder and lattice career paths[13]

Rather than being viewed as a gap or break in a career, maternity leave should be viewed as a pause, much like it would if someone were to be on a medical leave or education leave. Maternity leave, like many other career and life transitions, is a normal and healthy part of life.

LANGUAGE AND UNCONSCIOUS BIAS

As an employer, you are tasked with making a number of decisions each and every day. To filter incoming information, we often rely on mental shortcuts to help us organize and interpret information. These mental shortcuts are learned and ingrained in our thinking and become automatic. While efficient, they may not be accurate or effective, and may instead stem from unconscious biases. An **unconscious bias** is an assumption typically rooted in a stereotype or prejudice, which leads us to make uninformed and often inaccurate conclusions about a situation or another person. When left unexamined, unconscious biases can result in **micro-inequities** or actions that have a negative impact on you, your organization, and your employees. For example, you may assume all women want to take a yearlong maternity leave, and that family will always be their first priority. As a result, you unconsciously place them on a mommy track or in other words, a less intense, less demanding, and less ambitious career path. One way to combat both unconscious bias and micro-inequities is to employ simple, positive behaviours called micro-affirmations.

Micro-affirmations are subtle acknowledgments that recognize an individual's value and contributions (e.g., acknowledging a job well done or recognizing a skill or talent). When used consistently, micro-affirmations help us challenge our unconscious biases. As a result, this improves working relationships, and increases the receiver's level of self-esteem, performance, engagement, satisfaction, and commitment. In *What Works for Women at Work: Four patterns working women need to know*, Joan Williams and Rachel Dempsey identify four fundamental biases that affect working women:[14]

Prove it Again: Men are often promoted based on potential and women tend to be promoted based on performance, having to continually prove their competence through achievements before being promoted.

The Tightrope: The tendency to label agreeable and collaborative women as not assertive enough or too feminine, and to label assertive women as aggressive, not collaborative or too masculine.

The Maternal Wall: Expectations of working women that are based on their role as parents (i.e., commitment to their career *should* be lessened because they are mothers).

The Tug of War: All of the above biases combined, leading both men and women to judge and define the *right way* to be a woman and working mother.

Other Biases: taken from research in social psychology, that may impact working mothers include:

The In-Group Bias: Suggests we have a natural preference for others that are like us, whether they look like us, share the same interests, or have similar educational backgrounds and upbringings. With this bias, you may be more likely to hire or promote people like you and overlook those with different backgrounds.

Tips on preventing biases in the workplace:

- Avoid thinking in absolute terms. Words like always and never rarely leave room for exceptions, which do exist (e.g., working mothers always want part-time hours).

- Treat people as individuals, not as members of a group.

- Establish clear and transparent criteria for making decisions, such as hiring and promotion.

- Sponsor, coach and mentor employees not like you.

- Be proactive in identifying strengths in all your employees.

Recency Bias: The tendency to judge or predict someone's behavior based on recent events rather than long-term patterns of behaviour. For example, you may mistakenly assume that the birth or adoption of a child (recent event) will lessen a working mother's commitment, despite several years of work experience indicating otherwise.

Positional Bias: The belief that certain individuals are suited to specific positions. For example, you may believe that working mothers are best suited for administrative or customer service type work versus business development or leadership positions.

Confirmation Bias: The tendency to search for, and give more credibility to, information that confirms our opinions and beliefs. For example if you believe that working mothers demonstrate less ambition than other employees, it will likely be easier for you to seek out and recognize the information that confirms your belief, leading you to strengthen this bias.

As a human being, biases are inherent, and the term unconscious bias implies that you are unlikely to realize your biases and the behaviours that result from them. Employers have a responsibility to identify unconscious biases and understand the potential impact of their assumptions. From a business perspective, biases can be costly; when left unchecked, biases can result in lost talent or an ineffective use of existing and future talent. Biases can also lead to miscommunication, hurt feelings, disengagement, and sometimes formal complaints. With dedication and conscious effort you can address these tendencies and coach those around you to do the same.

A MODEL FOR EXPLORING UNCONSCIOUS BIASES

The following model will help you think about and challenge your unconscious biases. This can serve as a helpful exercise to guide your decision making process in the future.

Instructions: Take a moment to read through each section and jot down any thoughts that you may have. Feel free to discuss your responses and reactions with a trusted colleague or coach.

IDENTIFY	Identify one specific decision you have made such as a promotion, hiring, or appointment to a special project or committee.
ANALYZE	Ask yourself: What evidence did I collect and use to make my decision? Was my decision based on evidence or assumption?
SEEK FEEDBACK	Engage someone you trust, but who will also challenge you. Would they have made a similar decision? What information would they have taken into consideration? Do they think your decision was biased in any way?
EVALUATE	What impact does your decision have on how you see that individual or others similar to that individual? How does your decision influence the perceptions of others towards that individual? Can you recognize any micro-inequities you may have demonstrated (e.g., ignoring input from someone or overlooking the skills and talents of an employee)?
ARTICULATE	Is there an unconscious bias at work in this instance? If so, what is the bias? In what other situations might this bias operate?
COMMIT	Once you become aware of this bias, take steps to address it. Monitor similar situations that may be impacted by this bias. What micro-affirmations can you take to address the bias? Force yourself to play the devil's advocate when making future decisions.

Understanding Change and Transition
MATERNITY LEAVE CAREER TRANSITION

As an employer, it is not your responsibility to help a transitioning employee cope with *all* aspects of a transition. However, understanding the transition can help you gain perspective on potential challenges and opportunities. A model that is helpful to conceptualize this transition is one provided by William Bridges, who made a distinction between *change* and *transition*.[15]

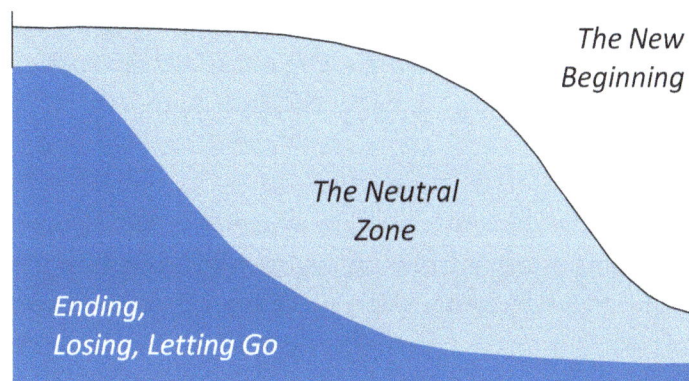

The New Beginning

The Neutral Zone

Ending, Losing, Letting Go

"So much of how a maternity leave unfolds depends on the individual manager, no matter how good or supportive the policies are. Your experience depends on the support you have at work. Everyone's maternity leave is different." – Employer Quote

The *change* is situational—the baby or adopted child is coming, the new mother will be away from paid work for a period of time. The *transition* is psychological—it is a three-phase process that people go through as they internalize and come to terms with the details of the new situation that the change brings about—the new mother will be temporarily uninvolved with paid work, a replacement needs to be found for the duration of the maternity leave or a team member may have to pick up the workload when an employee is not replaced.

Bridges' three-phase process includes: the ending, the neutral zone, and the new beginning. Although it may seem counterintuitive at first, the transition begins with an ending. The *ending phase* corresponds to the time before the employee begins her leave. During this time, organizations need to help employees (i.e., the employee going on leave, as well as her colleagues or direct reports) prepare for the change—the temporary absence of an employee's workplace, recruiting a replacement, and changes in workload. The organization can assist employees through this phase by providing information, identifying what will change, and accepting and acknowledging the emotions that may arise (e.g., excitement, anticipation, anxiety, and sadness).

The *neutral zone* corresponds to the time when the employee is on leave. During this time, the new mother will be adjusting to changes brought on by the new addition to the family and is unlikely to be involved in employment-related activities. Meanwhile, the employee's colleagues are adjusting to the absence of the employee who is on leave. Organizations can support employees during this phase by hiring a replacement, distributing the workload, and adjusting expectations.

Approaching the end of her leave, the employee may be feeling anxious about being out of the loop for a length of time. Organizations can start preparing the employee for her return by communicating changes that have occurred while she has been away. The reintegration of the employee into the workplace represents the third phase, the *new beginning*. The new mother may not be coming back to the same position she left, training may be required, or there may be new colleagues on the team. Laying out a step-by-step plan to reintegrate the employee will give everyone, including colleagues, a clear idea of their new roles and responsibilities, as well as any changes in processes and procedures.

Understanding Modern Working Mothers

A pregnancy or adoption is a time for celebration, as well as a time of change in routines, roles, and responsibilities. Women who are expecting may describe feelings of happiness, excitement, and amazement as they anticipate the arrival of their little one. However, there may be a wide variety of feelings, emotions, and psychological struggles occurring at every phase of the leave.

Specifically, for some women, positive emotions may occur simultaneously with feelings of anxiety. These feelings of anxiety may stem from anticipating the experience of becoming a mother or adding to her existing family, and all that is associated with this transition and this new part of her life.

"Maternity leave is a short period of time in the grand scheme of your employee's career. You can either damage that relationship, or truly solidify it in that time." – Employer Quote

---

Relatedly, an expectant mother may have concerns and trepidations about disclosing her pregnancy or adoption to her employer. There are many potential reasons behind this reluctance, including the fear that the employer will view the employee as less focused on her role and her long-term career overall. The employee may believe that her employer and colleagues will treat her differently due to the anticipated birth or adoption and her transition into motherhood.

As tasks within the usual scope of her paid role are reassigned to other colleagues in anticipation of her maternity leave, the individual may be concerned that she will be given less responsibility. Such inevitable necessities, though required, can create feelings of invisibility and a sense of dislocation for the expectant mother. However, not reassigning work until the last minute may impede the development of an adequate transition plan, potentially impacting the expectant mother and her colleagues by creating unnecessary stress through a less than adequate transition plan. The expectant mother may also fear that others will now view her as a short-term entity rather than a long-term asset within the organization, especially if others assume that she will not return to the workplace post-maternity leave. She may notice a growing sense of gradual invisibility, shifting from someone who was once valued within the organization to someone extraneous. The transition towards motherhood can create feelings of insecurity in a mother who perceives, accurately or mistakenly, that she is being excluded from long-term decision making within the workplace. She therefore may question her status and future prospects within the organization as a consequence of her maternity leave and impending absence from day-to-day activities.

If/when the mother returns to the workplace following her maternity leave, feelings of anxiety, insecurity, and lack of confidence may still be present. She may assume that her colleagues view her as a less productive member of the team due to her new responsibilities at home. The mother may also be toying with internal pressures as she feels the push and pull between home and work life. Her desire to be a good mother could potentially be competing with a professional desire to regain her status as a valued, respected employee, with a viable future within the organization. Some mothers might feel they are under extra scrutiny once again, believing that they need to rebuild their reputation, viability, and personal credit with their colleagues and employer as their situation has changed and they are now working mothers.

STRIVING FOR EXCELLENCE:
THE PUSH/PULL OF WORK AND HOME

Motherhood can be a profoundly transformative experience for women. Yet as a consequence of this transition and her shifting identity, a new mother may experience the internal pressure of being both a good mother and a good employee simultaneously. In other words, she may feel pressure to return to the workplace, and yet concurrently experience the guilt and anxiety related to her child attending childcare while she works.

Individually, the roles of a mother and an employee are both highly demanding. It can understandably feel overwhelming when the individual has both responsibilities to attend to, especially if she feels the internal and external pressures to be in both places, and to manage both roles, expertly. This can be challenging when the mother may also be carrying the guilt of electing to work in the paid labour force. Within the workplace, she may believe that she needs to prove herself once again as a valued employee, and demonstrate her commitment to her career and the organization. This may collectively lead to a psychological struggle as she works to reconcile both work and her new role as a mother. However, the drive or need to achieve both can be significant. And reasons may vary, from a desire to continue growing and developing in her career, to a need or desire to contribute financially to her household income, or even the consideration of her child's needs as he/she benefits from a developmentally rich childcare environment.

FEELING VALUED AND BEING APPRECIATED

Women who feel supported by their colleagues, and who have a chance to share their experiences openly, may experience less anxiety upon their return to the workplace. Observing fellow colleagues who may be experiencing the same challenges and experiences can also decrease the anxiety felt by mothers returning from maternity leave and increase feelings of inclusion in the workplace.

FROM MYTH TO REALITY:
EXPLORING COMMON BIASES TOWARDS WORKING MOTHERS

When we have limited information, we rely on heuristics to help us draw quick conclusions. These heuristics act as mental short cuts where we focus on one piece of a complex issue, rather than looking at the issue in its entirety. When we do this, we can make systematic errors in judgment. A reliance on heuristics may be one reason why stereotypes regarding motherhood persist in the workplace when they are largely inaccurate. Below, we debunk some common myths faced by working mothers:

Myth #1: Mothers put less effort into their jobs compared to fathers and non-parents

Intuitively, it may appear that working mothers are overburdened with several responsibilities both at home and at work. Therefore, employers might assume that work effort would suffer.

Reality: Motherhood does not predict effort at work.

In a study conducted by J. A. Kmec, employees were asked to identify how much effort they put into their workday; no difference was found in the reported work effort of mothers compared to that of fathers and childless workers.[16] In fact, mothers are not more likely to report that their responsibilities at home reduce the effort put in at work. Mothers are capable of adapting their home demands to meet, and exceed, their employer's needs. Even though they may have more household duties than fathers and non-parents, they are still very capable of effectively managing their time.

"Many people assume that mothers returning from maternity leave get less work done. Nothing is farther from the truth. If anything, I was re-energized. I let fewer people side track my day and work activities because I had to leave on time to pick up [my] kids. I feel I am more organized now with my work day than I was before kids." – Employee Quote

---

Myth #2: Mothers are distracted at work by thoughts of their children

There is a common misconception that working mothers only have kids on their minds, and that they have difficulty separating their work life from their home life. In other words, it is assumed that when working mothers are at home, they are thinking about work, and when at the office, they are consumed by thoughts of their children.

Reality: A woman's commitment to the organization is unrelated to her status as a mother.

In stark contrast, working mothers who participated in this research study actually reported that they "get so involved in [their] work that [they] forget about everything else, even the time."[17] Mothers work more intensely than childless women, and childless men exert similar levels of work intensity compared to working mothers.[18] Given this information, it is not surprising that a woman's commitment to the organization is unrelated to her status as a mother.[19]

In a survey of one thousand eight hundred practicing lawyers in Alberta, Canada, J.E. Wallace found that practicing lawyer mothers were more committed to their career than fathers, despite the fact that these women had less work control, spouses with longer work hours, and less support in the workplace compared to their male counterparts.[20] It is in the employer's best interest to have a workforce that is highly committed since it is positively related to a host of desirable behaviours, such as job involvement, job satisfaction and performance, and negatively related to such unwanted behaviours as withdrawal and turnover. [21]

Myth #3: Family responsibilities motivate fathers, but not mothers, to work hard

Historically, women were not expected to financially provide for their families in the same way that men did. As such, an assumption has carried forward that, although men are motivated to work hard in order to fulfill familial responsibilities, women are driven by more intrinsic factors, such as personal interest and achievement.

Reality: Family responsibilities tend to be highly motivating for both fathers and mothers.

Households with one breadwinner and one homemaker do exist, but they are becoming increasingly rare. With an increasing number of mothers working in either a part-time or full-time capacity, it is evident that working mothers are motivated to provide for their families. Both mothers and fathers are equally responsive to their breadwinning burden, and our survey responses showed that mothers feel motivated to provide financially for their family.

Myth #4: Women will not be as effective in the workplace after having children since they will not be working as much

From the perspective of some employers, having children is viewed as selfish since mothers will likely be more interested in putting time and effort into themselves and their family instead of their work. Also, employers fear that new mothers will not be at the office as much as they used to be, and they will no longer be as engaged in or committed to their work.

Reality: Quantity of work does not translate into quality of work.

Just because a new mother may not be in the workplace as often as she used to be does not mean that she will be disengaged in her work or less productive when she is in the office. Research shows that while new mothers tend to work less than before they had children, they are just as effective and productive in their jobs when at work.[22]

Rather than simply rewarding time spent at work, employers should focus their attention on what an employee is able to do in the time that she has; employers need to orient themselves not only with the quantity of work produced, but also the quality. In other words, do not manage by presenteeism but instead by outputs and goals achieved.

Myth #5: Creating work-life integration for mothers is not feasible

A common misconception is that a mother's family life will interfere with her work life. In other words, if an employee has to share time between her family and her job, she will be sacrificing some of the time that went into her work prior to having children. This leads to the assumption that once an employee has a child, she will automatically be less effective in her role at work.

Reality: Commitment to work and family is not a trade-off.

It is important for employers to understand that many of the people working for them, not just mothers, have important commitments and responsibilities outside of the office. Employees who feel that their employer supports them and is sympathetic to their personal lives are more likely to be satisfied, committed, and trusting of their organization. All employees, not just those with children, are likely to produce higher quality work at the office when they are able to commit time to their lives outside of work. While it may seem counterintuitive at first, employees who are able to spend quality time at home tend to be more productive at work, as they are likely to reciprocate that high level of quality when in the office. The age-old saying that "the busier you are, the more you get done" applies well to this situation.

To facilitate work-life integration, mothers often make adjustments to their lives by sacrificing leisure time in order to work better and harder. Mothers are aware of the biases that exist. Some mothers even fear letting their family responsibilities be publicized at work, and as such will often take extra care to integrate their responsibilities. This is actually beneficial to employers, given that mothers learn work-relevant skills such as multitasking, focus, organization, and creativity, as a result.[23] In addition, in order to create this integration, mothers are more likely than fathers to give up their leisure time, which creates more time for mothers to integrate home and work responsibilities.

Myth #6: New mothers are not interested in career progression

An assumption is commonly made that once women have children, they are no longer interested in progressing in their careers or pursuing a leadership track. Commitment that was previously given to their job is now presumed to be directed towards their child, detracting from the interest that they may have previously had to advance in their work.

Reality: An interest in career progression depends more on personal career ambitions than familial responsibilities.

Employers who were interviewed acknowledged that a new mother's engagement in her work is subjective and highly dependent on the needs and desires of the individual who is returning from maternity leave. In other words, one's own circumstances and preferences impact whether career progression is made. While consideration must be given to the potential limitations that she now has in terms of travel, overtime, etc., this does not necessarily mean that a leadership position is no longer of interest. Having an open and honest conversation with new mothers, upon their return to work, about career aspirations and goals is key.

Myth #7: Women on maternity leave do not want to be in contact with their employer

Often times and with the best intentions, employers make the assumption that a new mother who is on maternity leave will not want to be contacted by her employer while she is on leave. Given her additional responsibilities, employers may think that they are doing the employee a favour by letting her focus on life at home, without having to think about work.

Reality: Individual communication plans are key.

One of the most common fears expressed by new mothers is that they would be forgotten by their organization (i.e., out of sight, out of mind). While there is no right answer for how much communication is appropriate during the maternity leave, developing a communication plan prior to her departure is key. Having these conversations will allow for greater clarity and prevent unnecessary and potentially damaging assumptions. One focus group member spoke to her experience as an employer and indicated that, "Allowing the option for employees on leave to remain connected provides a positive impression that we still consider them to be an employee." Not only is this sense of inclusion important during the maternity leave, but it can also make the transition back to work easier and more seamless when those on maternity leave are kept up-to-date. Keep in mind that the communication plan you establish with your employee does not need to be complicated. A quick hello every couple of months, or a meeting for coffee, can go a long way in demonstrating to your employee that she continues to be a valued member of your team.

WHAT CAN EMPLOYERS DO?

It is possible that our stereotypes about working mothers may indirectly affect their career advancement.[24] However, the assumptions we hold about working mothers are far removed from actual working behaviour. Contrary to common beliefs, research indicates that working mothers have a unique ability to focus exclusively on job demands, while balancing their household responsibilities.

To counteract motherhood biases, it is necessary for organizations to directly address them. First, organizations can dismantle or challenge the sociocultural view of the ideal worker, which aligns with individuals who shoulder less responsibility outside of the workplace. Organizations often reward long hours and fixed schedules, but more attention should be given to tasks achieved. Although mothers can integrate the two roles, it is imperative that organizations remain realistic about work expectations. Special attention should be given to support working mothers, such as scheduling fewer meetings after working hours, and allowing a more flexible schedule, when possible. By doing so, organizations can demonstrate to working mothers that they are valued.

As J. A. Kmec indicated, increasing awareness is the first step in removing inequity.[25] By implementing policies to ban differential treatment on the basis of family responsibilities, organizational members can become more aware of the issues. To do so, it may be necessary to supplement *subjective* performance evaluations with *objective* criteria, when possible, or enhance accountability for decisions that are made. The biggest opportunity as an employer is to provide working mothers with relevant workplace support.[26]

Understanding Modern Employers and Maternity Leave

A PARADIGM SHIFT

What is it about the term maternity leave that carries negative connotations for some organizations? Medical leave does not necessarily carry the same stigma, yet can persist just as long, if not longer, than a maternity leave. Under these circumstances, employees often leave with limited notice and their return date is uncertain. It is important for organizations to put this notion aside, and halt the **motherhood penalty.** But how do organizations shift gears and turn maternity leaves from an inconvenience into an opportunity? Contrary to popular belief, maternity leaves can actually carry a host of opportunities and benefits for organizations.

"People need to treat maternity leave like any other type of leave. If we just changed our language and the way we talked about this type of leave, then it wouldn't be such a unique or female-only situation. If organizations didn't make such a big deal of mat leave and knew how to handle the transition better, it wouldn't be viewed so negatively. It's a leave, and it happens to coincide with the birth of a child, but it's not different from any other type of leave."
- Employer Quote

For instance, when an employee informs her employer that she will be taking a maternity leave, the organization's immediate concern can be, "Who will fill her position?" What organizations fail to utilize, at times, is their very own

31

candidate pool. A maternity leave is the perfect time to provide career progression or learning opportunities for another individual, or several individuals, within the organization. An organization has the opportunity to capitalize on placing existing employees in temporary roles to observe and assess whether they could be successful in that role in the future. When a full-time position then becomes available, the organization has a viable candidate that is already familiar with the position. Not only will the costs associated with training be diminished, but the organization may not have to expend costs and effort to recruit another individual.

Although it may sound counterintuitive, within the months that an employee adjusts to her role as a new mother, she will also grow in significant ways that will allow her to become a better employee. When a new mother has work responsibilities added to her home responsibilities, she becomes better able to manage her time and prioritize her workload. Rather than being consumed with thoughts of home life, which is a major concern for organizations, employees actually reported feeling more absorbed in their work. This is extremely beneficial to an organization, as they are often retaining an employee who will be focused and ready to face the challenges of their job. When viewed from these perspectives, employers are actually doubly benefiting by having a broadened applicant pool and a more highly skilled employee.

Organizations can also view the reintegration of an existing employee as an opportunity. Specifically, by being reintroduced to the organization, employers can be positioned to retrain the employee (i.e., new habits can be formed). Although this may come at a marginal cost, training a new employee would cost the organization substantially more (recruitment, advertising, training, etc.) than reintegrating an employee who is familiar with the role. Overall, there are many unfounded concerns regarding maternity leave. However, these problems should be viewed as possibilities, and maternity leave should be viewed as a pause, rather than an end, to a career.

"We need to consider [maternity] leave as a bigger concept, instead of just focusing on it being the woman's issue. This will allow for a wider acceptance and normalization of the process. Only then can we truly focus on what a maternity leave actually means. - Employer Quote

---

Before the Maternity Leave

Open and ongoing communication can contribute to a successful maternity leave transition for both the employee and the employer. It begins with that first communication, when the employee informs the employer of her pregnancy or intention to adopt. Employees are legally required to notify their employer a minimum of six weeks before the maternity leave begins. However, a supportive environment, where families, pregnancy, and adoption are celebrated, will help women feel more comfortable and able to talk about their pregnancy so that early disclosure is more likely. This allows for earlier and more effective planning, both in terms of the needs of the organization and of the woman taking maternity leave. Additionally, there is an opportunity to offer congratulations, find out how she is feeling, determine whether there are any concerns (e.g., safety, health), and discuss how she would like to communicate the news to her colleagues and other stakeholders.

It is important for employers to be aware that, for some women, discussing pregnancy or other family-related matters might be considered a private topic that they may feel uncomfortable having open conversations about in the workplace. Women from some cultures or faith groups might not disclose that they are expecting until late in the pregnancy and might not be comfortable discussing their pregnancy with a male employer, colleague, or customer/client at all. These factors should be considered as part of the first communication and appropriate accommodations implemented (e.g., have a female manager/HR advisor available to discuss pregnancy-related arrangements).

Once a manager is informed of the pregnancy/adoption, other parties who are responsible for managing HR practices should also be notified, so that the employee is provided with information regarding the organization's policies and procedures. If possible, provide an information package explaining what the expectant mother needs to do and what support is available from the organization. You can also include information on how to access government benefits, including maternity and parental benefits, as this can be a difficult system to navigate. Some employees may assume that the employer will facilitate this process, rather than realize it is an *employee driven* and *employer supported* process. Be sure to provide any supporting documentation (e.g., Record of Employment) in a timely fashion so as not to delay the employee's receipt of benefits.

Some leading practices for support during this phase include:

· Checklists to ensure clear, sensitive, two-way communication with an employee before, during, and after her return to work.

· Checklist for accessing and applying for financial benefits, including maternity/parental leave.

· Set up training to help support women before, during, and after maternity leave.

· Hold a pre-maternity leave workshop to allow staff to research options and hear about experiences of other working mothers in the organization.

· Offer pre-maternity seminars and health programs for women, with advice on nutrition, exercise, stress awareness, work/life integration, and possible childcare options.

· Set up a maternity **buddy system**, pairing those about to go on maternity leave with someone in a similar role who has already returned to work.

Measures should be taken specifically in respect to the following risks: arduous work involving manual lifting, carrying, pushing or pulling of loads; exposure to biological, chemical, or physical agents which represent a reproductive health hazard; special equilibrium; physical strain due to prolonged periods of sitting or standing, to extreme temperatures, or to vibration.

Source: *Manager's Handbook Canada Labour Code—Part II.*

SAFETY AND SECURITY

Once the employee notifies the employer of her pregnancy, a health and safety risk assessment should be conducted, if necessary. If there are no doctor-ordered restrictions, employers should not assume a woman is unable to perform her duties because of her pregnancy. Every woman experiences pregnancy differently. As an employer, you may make decisions on behalf of your employees that are based on good intentions, yet the effect that these intentions have on the employee and her career could actually be grounds for a formal complaint or discrimination. The effect, not just intention, of your decision must be given adequate consideration. Be careful not to make decisions on behalf of the employee, which may be based on unconscious biases (e.g., assuming she cannot lift any amount of weight). However, if there are concerns that workplace conditions pose a safety risk to the pregnant employee, this should be discussed with her immediately, and actions should be taken to mitigate risks or find temporary options to avoid the risks.

Pregnant employees may need short periods of time off work to see a doctor, or lengthier leaves because of pregnancy-related conditions like threatened miscarriage. In some cases, the time off work may be temporary, and a woman may then return to work until her maternity leave begins. In other cases, a woman may go directly from medical leave (e.g., doctor ordered bedrest) to maternity leave. If an employee needs time off work because of pregnancy, her employer has a duty to accommodate her.

ACCOMMODATIONS AT WORK

A health and safety risk assessment will help the employer determine what accommodations are needed to ensure the work environment is not a danger to the pregnant employee's health and safety and that of her unborn child. Ensure the employee is involved in discussions regarding any accommodations that will be made. She has a right to ask for a temporary transfer to another job or to have dangerous duties temporarily stopped. She also has a responsibility to explain exactly what kind of help and assistance she may require.

In collaboration with the employee, employers should seek creative and flexible responses to individual pregnancy-related needs.

Accommodation ideas to consider include:

Leading Practice Snapshot: Monsanto Canada is an agricultural biotechnology company with approximately four hundred employees. This company provides generous maternity and parental leave top-up payments to employees who are new mothers or adoptive parents (up to 90% of their salary for twenty-six weeks), and also offers a generous subsidy for in vitro fertilization when needed, up to $15,000. Employees can also integrate their working and personal lives through a variety of flexible work arrangements, including shortened and compressed workweek options, teleworking and reduced summer hours.

- · **Physical/Adaptability:** Strategies to meet physical demands—lifting aids, temporary reassignment of duties, reserved parking, stools, ergonomic chairs, reassignment to less physically demanding jobs, and alternate workstations.
- · **Time/Flexibility:** Scheduling of shifts—time off work for doctor's appointments, flexible start and end times, periodic rest, teleworking, a

less physically demanding shift, limited overtime, job-sharing, and flexible use of leave.

· **Environmental/Individuality:** Policy modifications—exceptions to a dress code, modified uniforms, and relaxed "no food or drink" and "no-sitting" policies.

CAREER DIALOGUES

Career dialogues are an important tool before and after maternity leave transitions and for employee development in general. Unlike annual performance appraisals, which typically focus on the evaluation of the individual's assigned duties and tasks, while noting areas of strength or areas for improvement, career dialogues are future-focused and highlight opportunities as well as possibilities. Career dialogues also present opportunities for the employer to gain more understanding and perspective regarding the employee's perception of her career, including motivations and goals. To maintain the momentum of a career dialogue, it should be regarded as something ongoing. Discussions should be held frequently, such as every quarter or as opportunity necessitates. These conversations should not be viewed as a "one and done" activity. If you have not engaged the expectant mother in these types of conversations prior to her announcement, this is a great time to start, and sooner is better than later.

According to Canada Labour Code: On the written request of the employee, employers must inform employees who are away on leave of every employment, training, or promotion opportunity that arises during the period of leave.

The Chartered Institute of Personnel Development provides a list of topics that can be addressed within a career dialogue, including the employee's:[27]

· Feelings about their current job and career situation

· Skills and development

· Values and work-life issues

· Potential within the organization and aspirations

· Job and career options both within and outside of the organization

In addition to these topics, in preparation for maternity leave, career dialogues can also include a:

· Transition plan for all current projects and responsibilities.

- Transition plan for returning from leave that aligns with the working mother's career plan. If the transition plan involves other stakeholders (e.g., job-sharing upon return to work), encourage the employee to contact stakeholders to discuss these arrangements prior to her leave.

- Discussion of how much the employee would like to engage in work activities while on leave (e.g., attending training sessions, professional development workshops, team meetings, and other staff events or celebrations).

- Discussion about processes and the office politics relevant to changing jobs, as well action planning through the identification and evaluation of potential career options, leading to a decision.

It is important to approach career dialogues with trust, respect, and compassion, as the employee might feel anxious about her future with the organization and as an expectant mother. Use this conversation as an opportunity to be supportive of any concerns the employee has with respect to how the maternity leave will affect her career development within the organization.

The following table is a list of strategies to facilitate effective career dialogues:

PROVEN POSITIVE	GOOD TO AVOID
Start discussions once you become aware of the upcoming leave to allow time for effective planning and transition.	Do not have the conversation too late. If the employee has to begin her leave earlier than expected, you might not have sufficient time to put plans in place.
Practice active listening. Show your interest in the conversation, listen carefully, and check that you understand what she is saying by reflecting back and paraphrasing in your own words.	Do not make assumptions. For example, it is common for employers to make assumptions about whether or not expectant mothers will return to work after leave. Employers should refrain from doing this.
In large and midsize organizations you can illustrate a range of career paths and options, and encourage the employee to speak with colleagues in other positions within the organization. In small organizations you can outline career development and advancement opportunities and discuss ways to reach personal and professional goals in the workplace.	Do not expect that the employee will follow the same path as other employees with the same job or as other working mothers. Remember that not everyone shares the same career aspirations, and that these can change over the course of a career.

PROVEN POSITIVE	GOOD TO AVOID
Provide information about options and resources available to the employee prior to the maternity leave and upon her return to work (e.g., flexible work schedules, job-sharing, mentors or maternity buddies).	Do not assume that the employee knows what information is available, where to find it, or who to get it from.
Discuss how much the employee would like to engage in work activities (e.g., training, team meetings) while on maternity leave and be prepared if plans change after the baby comes. While on leave, some women do not want to be engaged while others expect to be actively involved, yet both may change their minds once the baby arrives.	Do not pressure the employee to engage in work activities while on maternity leave or imply that her career will be negatively impacted if she chooses not to engage.
Discuss the return to work plan and recognize that it may change over time. Agree with the employee to revisit the work plan during the maternity leave and before transitioning back to work.	Do not expect the return to work plan to be a static document. For maximum effectiveness, the return to work plan should evolve with the changing employee and organizational circumstances.
Be honest about questions you are unable to answer (e.g., Will I come back to the exact same job?).	Do not make promises you cannot keep.
Give suggestions and recommendations. As an employer, you will likely have access to more information about new projects or services, so if it is alright to share this information then do so. It is impossible for an employee to identify an interest in something if she is unaware the opportunity exists or if she lacks the necessary information to make decisions.	Do not dismiss her ideas or force a career goal on to the employee that she does not buy into. In order to increase the likelihood of engagement and goal attainment, it is essential that the employee feels motivated to do something, and doesn't feel as though she should have to do it.

Points to discuss and documents to include:

- · Tell me about your short-term and long-term career goals?

- · Tell me how you see your career goals fitting in with your career plan?

- · Tell me how I can support you in achieving your career goals?

- · Tell me about the projects or tasks you have done that you are proud of?

- · Tell me about where you see your career path taking you? What career path(s) have you identified? What specific job roles within this path are you most interested in pursuing at this time, or when you return to work?

- Tell me about the activities you would like to be engaged in that would align with your interests?

- Tell me about the projects, committees, and responsibilities that allow you to work on your strengths, build your core competencies, pursue your passions, and bring you closer to achieving your career goals?

- Tell me about the skills you need to enhance, courses you need to take, experiences you need to have, opportunities you would like to seize, and the key relationships you need to develop or nurture to reach your career goals?

"What could really improve the [maternity leave] experience is having organized times to meet with [your] replacement in order to facilitate the transition." – Employee Quote

---

PREPARING FOR THE TRANSITION

Document the plans discussed during the career dialogue; this should include, but is not limited to, details, practical considerations, and actions to be implemented. Both the employer and the employee will then have a record of what they have agreed to that will help each party to achieve a smoother transition with minimal misunderstandings.

Transition discussions can also provide the employer with an opportunity to plan how the employee's responsibilities will be handled while she is on leave. The option chosen – hiring a replacement, distributing the work between remaining team members, or postponing project-related work - will depend on a number of factors, including the employee's position, the nature of the business, and the skill sets of other employees. Regardless of which option is chosen, involve the expectant mother in the decision-making process and take steps to capture and transfer the employee's knowledge before the maternity leave starts. Ideally, the transition will allow for an overlap of time both before and after the leave with any replacements, if this option is chosen. Prepare for the unexpected (e.g., if the employee needs to start her leave early or does not return to work following her leave) to ensure appropriate steps are taken to preserve and retain valuable organizational knowledge and technical experience.

UNDERSTANDING COLLEAGUE AND CUSTOMER REACTIONS

Consider how the transition and the leave will impact internal and external colleagues and customers. Respect confidentiality regarding when to disclose the pregnancy and upcoming leave to relevant third parties. Once the information is disclosed, steps can be taken to involve stakeholders in conversations regarding the transition, if relevant (e.g., whom customers will be able to contact while the employee is on leave).

Take the time to identify everyone that may be impacted by the upcoming transition. Once all stakeholders are identified, you and the employee can begin to develop a communication plan about what information will be shared, including a plan for transitioning colleagues into new roles and responsibilities in the absence of the employee. Ongoing communication between you, the employee, and stakeholders and colleagues will ensure that everyone knows what to expect and have an opportunity to provide input with planning.

Refrain from making assumptions about how others might feel upon learning the news of the employee's upcoming maternity leave. While some may experience frustration or anxiety over possible scenarios, others may wish to convey their support or participate in any planned celebrations. Communicate to stakeholders about the transition and how it will be managed. This will effectively manage any concerns that others might have. Discuss anticipated and actual responses with the employee so that you can work collaboratively to maintain stakeholder relationships.

Tips for conducting a pre-maternity leave performance review:

- Ensure that the employee is objectively assessed according to pre-determined and transparent criteria for her performance in the role.

- Obtain the employee's input as part of her performance appraisal.

- Avoid bell curve appraisals, which rank or compare employees against one another.

- Focus on outcomes over which the employee has control.

- Focus equally across the entire performance period, not just recent performance.

- Use concrete examples of behaviours to support your appraisal.

- When providing constructive criticism, listen to understand the employee's rationale for her performance.

- Be aware of biases you may have towards the employee that could negatively impact the performance appraisal.

"There is a sense that the maternity leave is a 'sacred cow' and you can't touch it or discuss it from an employer perspective, which is actually doing a disservice to the employee."
– Employer Quote

EXIT INTERVIEW

Conduct a pre-maternity leave **exit interview** for the purpose of gaining feedback. Include a dialogue regarding the quality of support and planning processes during the pre-maternity leave period.

Points to discuss and documents include:

- Tell me about the aspects of your job and the organization that you enjoy the most? Least?

- Tell me about the resources you need from the organization, your colleagues, and me to be successful in your position?

- Tell me how we can better support new and expectant mothers?

- Tell me how to communicate with and support new and expectant mothers to facilitate the maternity leave transition?

- Tell me how to improve your pre-maternity leave transition process?

- Tell me about what you need from your organization, your colleagues, and me, to ensure a smooth transition back into your role?

- Tell me about how our policies and procedures regarding maternity leave are currently stated and communicated, and how you think we can improve?

RETURN TO WORK PLAN

Ensure the **return to work plan** is in place before the leave starts to facilitate the transition back to the workplace. Although it may change over the duration of the maternity leave, having a basic plan in place ensures a smoother transition. Steps can also be made to adapt or modify the plan prior to the employee's return to work.

Points to discuss and documents include:

- Date of expected return.

- Employee responsibilities regarding notification of return to work (e.g., some policies require the employee to provide written notice six weeks prior to returning to work).

- The return to work plan can allow for weekly or biweekly reviews/meetings between the employer and employee after her return to help support the transition back to work. A formal review can also occur within the first couple of months of her return to review the employee's objectives and actions from the career dialogue conducted prior to her leave. It is a great opportunity to determine if these objectives are still relevant to the new mother.

· Maintain the communication plan for the duration of the leave (e.g., some employers use "keeping-in-touch" days to keep the employee up-to-date on organizational changes, training opportunities, or other work-related activities that the employee may wish to be involved in).

· **Re-onboarding** and reintegration actions (e.g., support, assessment of skills, safety orientation, and recertification, such as first aid). It is common for the returning employee to experience some anxiety about coping with both parenting and job responsibilities. The employer can set up a meeting with the employee upon her return to work to welcome her back personally. The return to work plan can also outline strategies to help the employee rebuild her confidence, such as regular feedback sessions and /or access to a coach or mentor.

· Career options (e.g., what positions may be available within the organization upon the employee's return).

· Work schedule options (e.g., soft return, or a graduated return, to full-time hours, flexible hours, or teleworking). A **soft return** is characterized by an agreed upon start and end time, but the employee may have a reduced or minimal workload the first few days or first week after return. A **graduated return** is characterized by regular responsibilities but a gradual increase in time at work each day or week until the target hours per day and week is reached.

· Roles and responsibilities (e.g., who is responsible for putting in place the different parts of the return to work plan).

· Handover (e.g., identify how the handover of responsibilities back to the employee will take place).

Employers play a key role in managing transitions and making the process a positive experience for new and expectant employees. Communicating support, engaging in career dialogues, and establishing a comprehensive transition and return to work plan will ensure the employee goes on maternity leave feeling valued and supported. Further, the new/expectant mother will be clear about what she needs to do, and how the organization will assist her, without any major concerns about her job, her career or her return to work.

"One practice I have struggled with is when annual performance ratings for women who were gone some portion of the year on maternity leave are too readily rated as N/A or receive an automatic 'middle of the road' rating without any real effort to assess based on actual performance. It feels to me like a systemic 'punishment' for being absent with the message that we can't be bothered to figure out how to fairly evaluate so we will default to giving you an average rating. This has a cumulative negative effect on a woman's career path and growth."
- Employer Quote

Sample Checklist – Before the Maternity Leave

- ☐ Upon the employee's announcement, follow the employee's lead and congratulate her if it makes sense to do so. Everyone reacts to pregnancy and adoption differently, so if you are unsure how to respond as an employer ask, "How do you feel about it?" as she announces her pregnancy.

- ☐ Determine if the employee has any specific accommodation requirements regarding her pregnancy.

- ☐ Provide the employee with an information package that explains what she needs to do and what support is available (e.g., the organization's maternity leave policy and procedures, flexible working policies, employee support networks, relevant external support available).

- ☐ If applicable, conduct a health and safety risk assessment.

Set up regular scheduled meetings to:

- ☐ Engage in career dialogue.

- ☐ Discuss any changes to health and safety and modifications to work accommodations.

- ☐ Discuss how the workload will be managed in her absence.

- ☐ Develop plans for a replacement/coverage if the position is being backfilled.

- ☐ Discuss what kind of contact the employee would like to have with you during her leave (e.g., you may plan times to have phone calls or send e-mails during her leave to keep her up-to-date on organizational changes). Clarify which e-mail address to use, especially if her work e-mail is being forwarded to a colleague.

☐ Conduct a performance review if the employee will be absent during a review period.

☐ Create a return to work plan, including the tentative date the employee expects to return, and the date the employee must notify the employer of her return.

"Having a plan to reintegrate employees back into the workforce so that they feel valued and are seen as valuable is essential." - Employer Quote

---

During the Maternity Leave

To avoid the risk of "out of sight, out of mind," you can provide the new/expectant mother with the opportunity to participate in events, such as team meetings, team building events, training seminars, or staff functions/parties. Some new mothers will appreciate the contact, while others may not, or they may not have the time and/or resources to do so (e.g., childcare).

While Canadian legislation permits employers to engage in reasonable contact with employees during maternity leave, the employee should be made aware that she is under no obligation to maintain contact with her employer.

"The most important thing is that the individual be taken into consideration. Some women want to stay in touch, some don't; some want to extend their leave; some can't wait to come back. A good program will involve connecting with women, talking about options, and giving her choices."
- Employer Quote

CONFIDENT COMPETENCE

Many women on maternity leave will report a loss of confidence when returning to work. It is a phenomenon that extends not just to women and maternity leave transitions, but to other types of leave, which cause someone to disengage from work for an extended period of time (e.g., medical leave, extended vacation, or sabbaticals). A working mother may even question her confidence when returning to a role that she has successfully performed for several years.

Albeit unfortunate, it is a common experience, and one that is rarely evidenced by a corresponding decline in skills and abilities.

In the book, *The Confidence Code: The science and art of self-assurance - What women should know*, authors Katty Kay and Claire Shipman explored factors associated with women's career success, noting that confidence is equally as important as competence.[28] Providing women on maternity leave with **professional development** opportunities can be one way to mitigate this concern upon reintegration. Professional development can also be critical in rapidly changing industries, such as technology and research and development, in which employees are constantly learning.

Employers can offer a range of learning opportunities to employees on maternity leave, such as webinars, distance courses, conferences, conference calls, and subscriptions to relevant industry publications, to keep them engaged in the organization and their own professional development. It is important to communicate that participating in these activities is voluntary. And, you may also want to consider reimbursing the employee for costs associated with participation (e.g., parking, travel, childcare).

COMEBACK COACHING

Organizations enlist the support of career coaches for a variety of reasons. **Comeback coaching** provides career transition support to mothers returning to employment after maternity leave or a more extended period of raising a family.

Career and life are inseparable and impact one another in a reciprocal manner. Every working mother experiences the return to work transition uniquely and could benefit from extra support from an objective and helpful third party. Comeback coaching can begin in the weeks prior to the projected date of return, and can continue into the first few months after the actual return, or as the particular situation determines.

Comeback coaching will allow the new mother to gain clarity on her career goals and can support her in re-establishing the career dialogue. It also sends a clear message to the new mother that she is a valued employee and that you are willing to invest in her development and support her reintegration into the workplace.

It can be difficult for many individuals (not just mothers), even those with extensive career and life experience, to identify or articulate career goals, which in turn makes it difficult for you, as the employer, to provide the means and support necessary to develop and leverage the strengths of the employee. Comeback coaching is a strategy that can have a positive impact for both the returning mother and the organization.

COMMUNICATING VALUE

Fostering a positive working relationship with your employee can also support her in developing confidence. Do not assume that your employee knows that she is competent or knows that you, her colleagues, or customers, value her skills and expertise. When presented with the opportunity to communicate with the employee on leave, be sure to take that time to express how much of an asset her skills are to the organization.

"I feel like I started a new job even though I came back in a job I have been doing for the past seven years." – Employee Quote

---

Enacting the Communication Plan

Although small changes may not seem like a big deal, such as where files are stored or what policies state regarding everyday processes (e.g., ordering office supplies), a number of small changes over the course of a year can be a lot of change to come back to all at once. It may seem trivial to communicate every single change with an employee who is on leave, but the employee's role could be impacted by any number of adjustments in the workplace and everyone responds to change differently. To help you decide on an appropriate way of managing this, refer to the employee's communication plan to determine what to communicate, who will update the employee, how the employee will be updated (e.g., phone, e-mail), and the frequency of contact. For example, you and your employee may agree to an e-mail update every two months for matters regarding administrative functions, but you may agree to updates within forty-eight hours for staffing changes or internal job postings.

Also, be open to changing the communication plan that was established prior to the commencement of the maternity leave. A new mother may find that the agreed upon communication plan may not be enough, or it may be too much. Check in with her to gauge if any adjustments are necessary by asking the following question: "Would you prefer more or less communication, or would you prefer something to be added or excluded from our communication plan?"

Sample Communication Plan

Name: _____

Date: _____

Preferred e-mail address: _____

Preferred contact number: _____

CHANGE	WHEN TO UPDATE	COMMUNICATED BY WHO	PREFERRED METHOD OF COMMUNICATION	UPDATE REINTEGRATION PLAN	DATE OF COMMUNICATION
Promotional and Training Opportunities	Within 48 hours	Manager or Supervisor	Phone	N/A	Jan 5, 2016
Administrative Processes (e.g., ordering supplies)	Every 2 months	Office Manager	e-mail	Yes, Meet with Office Manager upon return to clarify questions	Mar 10, 2016

Updating the Return to Work Plan

Workplace changes that have occurred while the employee is away on maternity leave may impact the employee's reintegration plan. For example, while on leave the organization may have introduced new software or may have new rules to comply with occupational health and safety. It is important to keep track of these changes that might necessitate re-orientation or re-onboarding. Also, remember that the working mother's plans may have changed; she may express interest in returning earlier than originally stated, she may delay her return, or she may not return at all. As an employer, your organization may have also experienced unanticipated changes (e.g., layoffs, restructuring) during the mother's leave. It is important to reconnect with the employee to communicate the information you have, given that you may have to adapt the return to work plan. Once the change and potential impact on the mother's role is identified, you will be in a better position to determine the appropriate next steps.

RETURN TO WORK LOGISTICS

Ensuring workplace logistics are in order will allow a smoother transition back to the workplace. Depending on the timeline for your organization's processes, you may want to think about getting necessary workplace logistics prioritized and initiated at least four to six weeks before the anticipated date of the employee's return.

Sample Checklist - During the Maternity Leave

- ☐ Send flowers and congratulatory note on behalf of the organization.
- ☐ Contact employee as per pre-arranged communication plan to:
  - ☐ Inform of any changes/updates within the organization.
  - ☐ Inform of any relevant work activities, training, or celebrations taking place within the organization.
  - ☐ Discuss the return to work plan and her role upon return (this should take place closer to the return to work date).

Sample Checklist - Return to Work Logistics

- ☐ Keys and passcodes to access worksites, filing cabinets, storage rooms, security alarms, computer programs
- ☐ Work ID
- ☐ Office supplies
- ☐ Safety equipment
- ☐ Communication devices, telephone, cell phone, voice mails, laptops, computers
- ☐ Workspace
- ☐ Uniform
- ☐ Locker, storage space for personal items

- ☐ Professional registration
- ☐ Insurance for vehicles
- ☐ Professional licenses, certifications
- ☐ Parking pass
- ☐ Other_____
- ☐ Other_____
- ☐ Other_____

Inform colleagues and other employees of the working mother's return date, encouraging them to provide support during the reintegration phase. Be sure to designate someone to meet the returning mother at the beginning of her scheduled start time to officially welcome her back.

Post-Maternity Leave/Reintegration

When the working mother returns to paid work, you have a great opportunity to facilitate her transition back to the organization and implement strategies that will allow her to continue to perform to her full potential. Adopt a transition mindset and explore a variety of options to successfully integrate the working mother back into the role, her team, and the organization.

"Returning from maternity leave I was ignored. I was in a weird zone where I wasn't treated like a new employee (onboarding) and I wasn't treated as a valuable asset. I was out of the loop and not immediately useful. I felt like an afterthought that nobody cared about." – Employee Quote

RETURN TO WORK INTERVIEW

Much like the exit interview you conducted prior to the maternity leave, once the mother returns to work you are presented with a similar opportunity for conversation. Depending on when you last discussed the return to work plan, you might consider having this discussion after the working mother has been in her role for at least a month. It is important to provide the returning employee with sufficient time to get a feel for what some of her challenges might be, if any. However, you do not want to leave too large of a gap between the actual return date and this conversation, in case there are some concerns with the return.

This conversation is a great time to re-engage and continue the career dialogue, assess how the reintegration is going, and determine what further support and assistance may be required (i.e., a re-orientation like you would provide for a new employee). Some sample questions may include:

- What have been the best or most satisfying aspects of returning to work?
- What have been the most challenging aspects of returning to work?
- Will you need additional support and resources to be successful in returning to work?
- How else can I, or others, support you in your role?

Keep in mind that even the most experienced working mother can feel unprepared to deal with all the nuances of career, life, and family, but with your patience, understanding, and support, you and your employee will achieve both of your goals quicker and with increased satisfaction.

"When I returned from maternity leave, I felt displaced. Yes, my 'job' was secure, but many of my responsibilities were transitioned to other employees and were not returned to me. There was no re-orientation, and no one had the time to spend with me. At best, I felt that I had returned to a placeholder position with an empty title, but certainly not as the contributing, valued member of the team I had been previously and was eager to be again." – Employee Quote

PROMOTING MENTORSHIP AND SPONSORSHIP

A working mother can greatly benefit from mentorship and sponsorship opportunities. Although we have previously noted the use of the buddy system, this strategy may be specific to a certain life occurrence (i.e., maternity leave career transition), while mentorship and sponsorship can be enacted at any point in the working mother's career, independent of maternity leave career transitions. Although both mentors and sponsors support the working mother's career development, the nature of each relationship is unique.

Mentorship is a developmental relationship where one individual with more knowledge and experience guides the lesser experienced individual.

Mentors are often:

- Internal or external to the working mother's place of employment
- Aware of the working mother's career and life goals
- Functioning in an advisory or coaching role
- Indirectly responsible for the career advancement of the working mother

By contrast, **sponsorship** is characterized by the working mother having an ally (usually a more senior employee) in the organization who has the power to effect change and actively advocates for career building opportunities.

Sponsors (or advocates) are often:

- Internal to the organization or the working mother's professional community
- Aware of the working mother's career and life goals
- Advising on relevant career opportunities
- Directly responsible for the career advancement of the working mother
- Advocating for specific assignments or promotions on behalf of the employee

While both mentorship and sponsorship can support the development of a working mother's career, there are several unique benefits related to sponsorship that benefit both the employee and the organization.[29] Specifically, sponsorship can:

- Identify and accelerate the careers of high performers within the organization
- Assist working mothers to address specific challenges within their roles
- Challenge and address lower female representation at senior levels within an organization by supporting the career development of women
- Improve the working mother's level of reported career satisfaction and organizational commitment
- Lead to higher-performing teams and leaders
- Lead to increased diversity at senior levels

Sample Checklist – Post-Maternity Leave/Reintegration

☐ Ensure buddy system and/or comeback coaching is in place, if using.

☐ Provide a mini reorientation to the workplace to introduce any changes that have occurred during her absence (e.g., changes in policies, procedures, new team members)

☐ Re-establish the career dialogue and revisit the employee's career goals

Customization of Career Path
ALTERNATIVE/FLEXIBLE WORK ARRANGEMENTS

To date, Canada provides job protection status for female employees on maternity leave (not contractors), but does not have any policy mandating **flexible work arrangements** for working mothers.[30] Work-life integration is identified as one of the biggest problems that new mothers face when returning to the workplace, and as a result it is critical that employers consider the value of offering flexibility or alterative arrangements into the work schedule.

As an employer, there are a number of options available to you when offering alternative/flexible work arrangements to working mothers. Below we have included the common alternative approaches that might suit your work environment and the needs of your employees, which include: telework/WORKshift, part-time work, flexible hours, and job-sharing.

"Companies need to be flexible when dealing with individuals on maternity leave. A 'one size fits all' approach does not work for everyone." - Employer Quote

---

BENEFITS OF FLEXIBLE WORK OPTIONS

As Canada continues to face a labour market shortage and a labour skills mismatch, the ability of employers to retain staff, and demonstrate a willingness to enact flexible work arrangements, becomes increasingly important.[31] Women and mothers play an integral role in the modern workforce, and are key players to address this labour market shortage. Employers who neglect to consider and address the importance of work-life integration may put their organization at risk.

Some of the benefits of offering flexible work arrangement to both employees and employers include:

More satisfied employees: Encouraging work-life integration directly influences employees' perceptions of workplace support. Employees who feel appreciated also tend to be more satisfied.

Retained talent: Employees who continue to work after maternity leave are often well versed in the demands of their work role. Employers can save a great deal of time and money by retaining skilled employees.

Better team dynamics: Employees who work for an organization that values work flexibility are more likely to be connected as a group, invested in the well-being of others, and supportive of each team member's personal commitments.

Increased productivity: Improved morale, loyalty, and engagement, as the result of workplace flexibility, leads to increased performance and levels of productivity in staff. When employees are afforded the opportunity to work where and/or when it best suits their personal working style, they are likely to produce higher quality work. Employees who are able to commit more time to their lives outside of work are also likely to reciprocate this dedication when at the office.

Lowered environmental impact: Some flexible work arrangements allow employees to work from home, meaning that less time is spent commuting to and from work. According to the Canadian Telework Association, if one million teleworkers were to work from home one day each week, fifty million hours of time would be saved.[32] Other benefits include significant reductions in carbon dioxide emissions, fuel costs, and mileage.

When creating a distributed team, consider the following:

- Context: What is the purpose of the team?

- Mission and Objectives: What is the team setting out to achieve?

- Composition and Roles: What knowledge and skills do you need on your team to accomplish your goals?

- Authority and Boundaries: What are the roles and responsibilities of each team member?

- Resources and Support: What are the resources available to the team to support the attainment of the identified goals?

- Operations: How will the team operate (e.g., hours of work, meetings)?

- Negotiation and Agreement: Consensus regarding the charter is achieved.

Adapted from MindTools.

Reduced turnover and hiring costs: Improving recruitment and retention is critical for organizations given the high cost of replacing employees, including recruitment, onboarding, and training. A recent study found the average cost of replacing employees to be approximately 40% of the annual salary for entry-level staff, 150% for mid-level employees, and up to 400% percent for specialized or high-level employees.[33]

Improved morale and commitment: Flexible work arrangements increase the number of employees who intend to stay with the organization, with many mothers expressing an increased likelihood of returning to work if they will be provided with flexible work options. [34]

Reduced stress: New mothers who have the opportunity to integrate their work and home lives experience less strain, reducing overall stress and fatigue. This brings a number of benefits to the organization, including increased productivity, motivation, and engagement.

Agile infrastructure: If coordinated properly, having employees with alternative schedules can also allow for more efficient use of your office by sharing space, supplies, and equipment between staff, thereby reducing real estate and associated costs.

Reduced absenteeism: Employees who have better work-life integration are shown to benefit from reduced levels of stress and demonstrate greater overall mental and physical health. As a result, employees are more predictable and have a reliable presence.

"Additional flex days before maternity leave to manage illness and flex days or teleworking options after returning from a maternity leave would significantly lower child care costs, co-ordination stress and loss of productive time for mothers. It would also lower pressure for parenting partners to also take sick days from work due to sick kids." - Employer Quote

---

TELEWORK AND WORKSHIFT

Telework and **WORKshift** involve working away from the traditional office space so that an individual is able to work when, where, and how they are most effective and efficient. Note that telework is one aspect of WORKshift, but not the only form of flexible work covered by this concept. Working when and where one is most effective, whether it be from home or other locations, and flexing one's hours are both part of this alternative way of working. For more information about WORKshift and how to integrate flexible work options within your organization, please visit www.workshiftcanada.com.

WORKshift arrangements can be a win-win situation for both employers and working mothers, when implemented correctly. For organizations, WORKshift arrangements allow employers to cut expenses incurred through operating costs and dedicated workspace. Employers who offer WORKshift arrangements are also seen by their employees as demonstrating a high level of innovation and leadership, which are traits that are highly valued by employees. For working mothers who struggle to facilitate an integrated lifestyle when returning to employment, having the ability to work from alternative locations is an attractive option. New mothers who work away from the traditional office are shown to be more productive, motivated, and efficient, often contributing back to the organization a large portion of what would be time spent commuting. [35]

It is important that you have a conversation with every mother who is considering working outside the traditional office about your expectations as an employer and the options available to her as an employee.

"Organizations can help with providing the opportunity to telework so that [new mothers] don't have to lose touch either during maternity leave or if they need to take a day off to tend to a sick child." - Employer Quote

---

Tips for Effectively Managing Mothers Who WORKshift

Create room for autonomy: Establish boundaries and constraints, but provide flexibility for WORKshifting mothers to define their own communication and reporting practices. Part of managing a successful WORKshift arrangement is allowing your employees the freedom to work in ways in which they are most motivated and productive. By adopting flexible work policies that place these employees at the center of their own decisions, you will further foster the performance of your working mothers.

Manage deliverables, not activities: When mothers are working from a distance, breaking down projects or assignments into concrete deliverables will allow both you and your employee to keep better track of performance and progress. Integrating tangible goals and outcomes into deliverables also provides the added clarity that is sometimes needed in remote work.

Engage in more frequent performance management: When you are not seeing your employees as frequently, it can be easy to neglect standard practices, like performance reviews. To avoid this, try having frequent and informal discussions with employees about their performance goals, and your expectations for them. This will not only strengthen communication, but also create better work performance outcomes.

Offer your complete trust: Until there is a concrete reason to assume otherwise, offer working mothers who are working away from the office your complete trust. Working mothers often feel judged when working from home. Although teleworking should never be a substitute for childcare, co-workers may view the mother as being with her children rather than working when at home. Giving her your trust will not only strengthen your professional relationship, but also motivate her to uphold an accountable and consistent reputation.

Be flexible in your management style: Be open to adapting your management style to match the needs and preferences of your employee. Understanding what enables a WORKshifting mother to perform at her best will not only maximize her efficiency, but also her engagement and commitment to the organization.

Leverage technology: Technology makes WORKshift arrangements feasible, and helps to support and manage teleworkers.

Considerations to Make Before Offering WORKshift Arrangements:[36]

Who will be responsible for health and safety issues and worker's compensation if the employee is injured while working away from the office?

While the health and safety considerations made for teleworking employees will differ from those in the traditional office environment, these employees should not be subjected to reduced health and safety standards. Employers are encouraged to collaborate with HR and mothers in teleworking roles to form a written agreement that clarifies these matters.

Who will buy and maintain the equipment used from home and what expenses will be reimbursed?

It is typical for employers to cover any expenses incurred by a teleworking employee that would normally be covered by the organization if said employee was working in the office (e.g., office supplies, computer software). Other costs to consider include telephone lines, Internet access, and travel time.

What hours will the employee be available to work?

WORKshifting employees often have the freedom to follow a more flexible work schedule. This may be appealing to new mothers who have other responsibilities during regular, nine to five, work hours. However, employers should not expect employees who work from home to be available at all times. Employers are encouraged to setup a communication plan with WORKshift employees to identify when they are available to work, take calls, and answer e-mails. A distributed team charter is recommended to set expectations around how the team will work together. This document can contain expectations for response times, handling conflict, what communication media to use for which purposes, and other topics.

How will overtime be approved?

It is important that employees who work from home (or elsewhere) have a strategy for keeping track of their hours. Whether this is through recording time on a tracking sheet or using time tracking software, having a dialogue about options for reporting work hours is important. Additionally, employers should have a conversation with their WORKshift employees about the number of hours that an employee should be working each day, length of breaks, lunches, etc.

How will communication between the teleworker, co-workers, supervisor, and/or customers be determined?

With teleworkers working away from the office, it can be more difficult to get in touch with them. It is important to collect personal contact information and keep this information on file. Having alternative ways of communicating is also beneficial (e.g., Skype chats and e-mailing). Whichever method(s) you choose, be sure to mutually assess and streamline communication preferences, and clarify when an employee is able and expected to be available to respond to messages. For communication regarding team projects or meetings that require more thorough instruction or collaboration, consider project sharing programs/software and shared drives that allow you to edit web-based documents and presentations using screen sharing tools.

How will work assignments, due dates, and work expectations be communicated?

Whether it is through weekly e-mail updates, daily phone check-ins, or another form of communication, establish a means of discussing progress with your WORKshifting mother. This not only provides you with greater clarity on the status of work, but also helps your WORKshifting mother maintain productivity and motivation. Establish whose responsibility it is to maintain this communication and monitor outcomes. A great way of managing work expectations is to share web calendars that allow you to post and track tasks or assignments.

PART-TIME WORK

An employee is considered to work **part-time** when they work less than thirty hours per week.[37] The number one reason mothers in Canada do not return to employment after being away on maternity leave is because there is a lack of access to part-time positions in their workplace.[38]

When new mothers have the opportunity to work part-time, they report less work-to-family strain. This is beneficial to their personal lives and professional lives as it allows new mothers to be fully present, invested, and alert in both roles. As an employer, knowing when and how to offer alternative work schedules to your employees that create opportunities for better lifestyle fit will serve you well in terms of retaining talent and maintaining commitment from employees who contribute to the organization. [39]

New-Concept Part-Time Employment

Working mothers can be hesitant to take up part-time employment because of the reduced compensation, marginalization on the job, and reduced career advancement opportunities that tend to be associated with these positions. To avoid this stigmatization, consider offering your employees what is known as **new-concept part-time employment** options. These positions often come with enhanced prestige, job satisfaction, higher income, and career opportunities for women.

Additionally, these positions often allow working mothers to maintain pro-rated professional salaries and benefits. These employment opportunities allow employers to retain talented and skilled workers while simultaneously encouraging mothers to develop in their career.

Tips for Effectively Managing Mothers Who Work Part-Time

Understand that integration is also about business: It might appear that offering a working mother reduced work hours is more of a favour than anything, but in today's fast-paced economy, a major source of success for businesses is the ability to be adaptable and agile, as well as to attract, retain, and develop key talent.

Provide mutual flexibility: Reduced hours work best when both parties are committed to the arrangement. As an employer, it is important that you honour the arrangement made with your part-time employee. If there are cases when an employee is needed outside her reduced schedule (e.g., for a meeting), flexibility must be given and received from both sides to effectively deal with the circumstances.

Focus on results gained, not time lost: Rather than focusing on the time lost from this employee, focus instead on the gains for the business, employee, and customers or clients. Often, working mothers who have more time to commit to their families are also more committed to producing quality work when on the clock. Focus your attention on what an employee is able to do in the time that she has, orienting yourself not only to the quantity of work produced, but also to the quality.

FLEXIBLE HOURS

Flexible hours involve a schedule where an employee works a full day but can vary her hours, allowing flexibility in the start and end of the work day.

- **Core time:** Hours of the day that employees are required to be at the office or otherwise accessible (e.g., 10:00 a.m. to 3:00 p.m.).

- **Flex time:** Hours of the day that employees have flexibility in when they can work.

Offering flexible hours to new mothers can be a useful alternative when they need to manage the multiple responsibilities of work and home life. For example, there may be time conflicts in daycare drop-off and pick-up that make it difficult for working mothers to work standard hours.

Not only do initiatives such as flextime offer more opportunities for employees to attend to other areas of their lives, but they also have positive impacts on their perceptions of the work environment, which leads to improved organizational outcomes.[40] As an employer, offering flexible hours also means that you will have the opportunity to improve coverage or extend the service hours of your business, allowing you to schedule work across longer portions of the day.

Tips for Effectively Managing Mothers with Flexible Hours

Maximize face time: When employees work flexible schedules, you may only get to see or touch base with them periodically, and the working mother may feel distant from the organization and other staff. If you notice that you are not seeing this employee as often as you would like, schedule time when you are both in the office to discuss work and other topics.

Implement an employee-centered strategy: Flextime has the most positive outcome for both employees and employers when it is based on an employee-centered strategy.[41] **Employee-centered strategies** emphasize a collaborative and participatory approach between all parties with an organization, which support employees to become as effective as possible through company programs, processes, and policies. Employee-centered strategies recognize and place value on the unique talents and circumstances of each employee. When considering flextime options, base your decisions on quality enhancement, cooperation, employee involvement, and participation, as opposed to reducing labour and other costs.

Keep flexibility consistent: It is important not to confuse a flexible schedule with a casual schedule. Employees with flexible schedules should be held to the same standards as other employees in terms of punctuality and dependability.

Considerations to Make Before Offering Part-Time Work or Flexible Hours

Are your employees going to be working core hours/days?
Employees with flexible or part-time hours may be given more leniency to determine their work hours. However, there may be core hours during the busiest points of the day where all employees are expected to be in the office. The length and time of lunch periods and breaks should also be negotiated with employees who are not in the office as often or during flexible times.

Are there certain times of the year when flexible arrangements are not viable (e.g., peak season or year-end)?

If you are unable to offer flexible arrangements to your working mothers during certain times of the year, make sure that this is communicated well in advance.

What time will your employee start and finish work? Will this schedule be consistent on a daily or weekly basis?

While flexible and part-time hours give employees the opportunity to vary their work hours, it is usually best to maintain consistency in the employee's schedule by establishing set times where she is expected to be available. You should agree on how long this modified schedule will be in effect, and it should be clearly communicated to the rest of the staff.

How will you ensure coverage of an employee's role if they are not available at the start or end of the business day? What arrangements will be made if questions arise in the employee's absence?

If an employee is not physically present in the office, make sure that another employee is available to cover the position if needed. You should also discuss whether it is necessary for her to be available to answer calls, in the case of an emergency, while she is out of the office.

JOB-SHARING

Job-sharing is an alternative work schedule where two employees voluntarily share the responsibilities and time commitment of one or more positions or sets of duties.

Creating opportunities for job-sharing has many benefits for your organization and your employees. According to a UK study, 90% of new mothers cited the option to job-share as being a potential factor in whether they would stay in or leave an organization.[42] This not only allows you to retain high-performing employees seeking flexibility, but also saves you the costs of recruitment and training due to turnover. In many ways, two heads are better than one, and this is also true of job-sharing.

Having two people working in one position could mean double the talent.[43] When there are two sets of perspectives brought to one position, a wider range of talent and experience can be drawn upon. Having two people responsible for the same job also creates a built in check-in system, with each employee being accountable to the other, thereby maintaining quality control and preventing errors on the job. Job-sharing also means continuous job coverage during vacation, sick leave, and other absences. However, absenteeism is unlikely to be a problem among job-sharing employees, who tend to experience less strain of balancing work and family responsibilities, contributing to greater overall well-being.

Tips for Effectively Managing Mothers Who Job-Share

Match skill sets: Ensuring that there are complementary skills, experiences, and perspectives in a shared position is important to establish flow and cohesion.[44] Job-sharers should also work well together on a personal level, and it is often beneficial if the two employees are in similar situations (e.g., both recently returning to work from a leave).

Be explicit: Make sure that you provide detailed job descriptions (ideally with the input of the two job-sharers) that identify each job responsibility, when it occurs, and who will be responsible for it. It is also important to be explicit with the rest of your team about which work responsibilities each employee is responsible for so that it is clear whom to report to or delegate work to.

Keep communication open: Maintaining communication with each job-sharer is key. It will be important to identify how each employee will be accountable for the work being done (i.e., either as a unit or individuals), and whether meetings and evaluations will be conducted one-on-one or together. Some organizations find that job-sharers are more accountable and committed to producing quality work when both employees are held jointly responsible.

Maintain some overlap: It is strongly recommended that at least a few hours of overlap time is scheduled each week between job-sharers so that the details of their work can be discussed/shared. This will allow for better organization and efficiency in the role, as well as enhance the communication between job-sharers.

Considerations to Make Before Offering Job-Sharing

How will the duties and responsibilities associated with the job be divided between employees?

Consider how the requirements of the position will be divided between your employees. Will it be divided based on tasks, workload, or days of the week? Are there any responsibilities that will be shared? Some job-sharers might be more comfortable having complete responsibility for certain tasks, while others will want to share the workload and prefer that no task be managed solely by one partner. The model that you choose will depend on the nature of the job and the preferences and skills of each employee. Make sure that the way in which job tasks are divided is explicit and specific in order to avoid any confusion.

What time will your employees start and finish work? What days of the week will each employee be in the office?

Consider whether your job-sharing employees will, if at all, split their schedules (e.g., morning and afternoon, daily, or weekly). When establishing a job-share schedule, make sure that you also consider how much overlap time is required.

How will holidays and time off (coverage) be managed?

When an employee is taking a short period of time off, it is nice to have another employee who is versed in their job to take over the responsibilities. However, covering extended holidays or extended time off can be more challenging when it comes to job-sharing. Rather than overburden the other job-sharing employee, be sure to consider alternative arrangements for coverage during these times.

Is the position suited to the restructuring necessary for job-sharing?

Some roles are easier to share than others. Positions well suited to job-sharing are those in which there is a clear division of responsibilities or tasks. Before offering a job-sharing opportunity to your employees, make sure that it is feasible to divide the work between two people.

Does your organization have the space and equipment necessary to accommodate two employees in one role?

If there are times when both job-sharing employees will be in the office together, it is important to consider whether your workplace has the space to accommodate them. Having two people carry out one role can also mean twice the equipment or supplies (e.g., computers, software, desks, telephone lines).

Leading Practice Snapshot: The University of Toronto employs approximately nine thousand full-time and over ten thousand part-time staff. They provide generous maternity and parental leave top-up payments for employees who are mothers, fathers, or adoptive parents, and all programs include same-sex partners. They also manage onsite daycare facilities at each campus location, which employees can take advantage of when they are ready to return to work, as well a generous offsite daycare subsidy, up to $2,000 per child.

Additional Considerations to Make Before Offering Alternative Work Arrangements

- Is offering an alternative work arrangement consistent with your organization's policy?

- How long will this modified work arrangement be in place?

- How and when will you review the modified work arrangement with your employee(s)?

- Will these arrangements be available to all employees, employees in particular departments, or only in special cases? How will you manage these conversations if they come up with other members of your staff?

- How might this modified work arrangement impact an employee's benefits and qualifications for government programs?

- What accommodations will be made if meetings, training sessions, or other important events do not fit with the employee's alternative schedule?

- How will you contact this employee if she is not in the office?

- What impact will this modified work arrangement have on the employee's future career development and progression with the organization?

Offering alternative work arrangements can be of great benefit for both working mothers and employers. While policies for enacting flexible work are typically decided upon within an organization, Provincial Human Rights Codes require employers to consider whether they can accommodate changes in an employee's schedule up to the point of undue hardship.[45]

We encourage you to take the time to think about whether offering alternative/flexible work arrangements for your staff might be a feasible option for your place of work. It can also be of value to think of these options as temporary or a gradual return to a regular work schedule. At the end of the day, make sure that whichever arrangement you choose is a good fit for both you and your employee and is developed collaboratively between the two of you.

Considerations for Diverse Populations

In 2013, 77% of all recent mothers were eligible to receive maternity and parental benefits; however, 33% of the population still remains unaccounted for.[46] This is a solid indication that not every mother-to-be equally benefits financially from maternity leaves. However, certain challenges transcend financial considerations and some groups will have to face unique circumstances and challenges both before and after giving birth.

"Going on maternity leave is still considered career suicide in my industry."
– Employee Quote

This begs the questions: Who are these individuals, and what distinctive obstacles do they face? Not surprisingly, most **marginalized mothers** are less likely to fully capitalize on their benefits for a host of reasons. These marginalized mothers include: young mothers, first time mothers over the age of forty, adoptive parents, aboriginal women, recently immigrated mothers, and same-sex mothers. In noting the previous, we also recognize that there are many other mothers not typically considered marginalized who also do not fully benefit from receiving employment insurance following a birth or adoption (e.g., some self-employed women, women working part-time, contract workers and consultants, and mothers already out of the workforce with another child). In the following sections, we outline some of the barriers some groups must surmount, and provide suggestions to employers on how you can provide assistance, when possible. This is an important issue to discuss given that the availability of job protected leave is a key factor in determining whether women will return to work after childbirth.

FIRST TIME MOTHERS UNDER AGE TWENTY-FIVE

Consideration 1

Young mothers (under twenty-five years of age) often have to deal with a number of issues from the onset of their career. Employers may be hesitant to hire young women, or worse, they may let them go before their maternity leave starts.[47]

Some employers fear that young women are more likely to leave during their work term to take a maternity leave. This may be a cost they are not willing to incur, given that they may have to pay for the recruitment, interview, and training of a new employee while the new/expectant mother is on maternity leave.

Consideration 2

A young mother's employer may stray from the traditional. Many young mothers are also students and, therefore, their schools will act as an employer and grant them maternity leave. This is an issue that rarely gets discussed. Young mothers have a heightened risk of remaining in poverty, because of the little social support they receive (i.e., from both families and the community), and it is imperative that they are given the resources to be successful in school. Generally, the risk of poverty decreases with increasing education. Academic institutions are encouraged to make young pregnant women aware of their options, and provide them with feasible alternatives for managing their education after the birth of a child.

FIRST TIME MOTHERS OVER AGE FORTY

Consideration 1

The demographic composition of first time mothers is changing. The percentage of first births for women who were thirty-five years or older has increased dramatically.[48] The proportion of women completing higher education has also increased, which can provide insight into why women are choosing to give birth later in life.[49] In the coming years, this will likely be the prevailing trend in motherhood. Generally, given the employee's presumed financial stability, employers may assume a woman who has a child at a later age, might take a longer maternity leave. This may pose a concern for employers who will have to replace these women for the length of their maternity leave. However, women who give birth later in life are more likely to have completed schooling, as well as have a greater accumulation of work experience, compared to their younger female counterparts, and may face a variety of pressures in deciding how long of a maternity leave to take.

Consideration 2

When women choose to get pregnant later in life, an unfortunate, yet very real consequence is that these women may have trouble conceiving. Some women will struggle with fertility treatments before they are able to conceive. Older mothers also tend to have more difficulty during gestation and delivery, have a higher risk of birth defects, and are more likely to have complications after delivery.[50] Employers must be aware of these issues and may have to allot extra time for appointments and sudden leave during pregnancy. It is also imperative for employers to exercise sensitivity when dealing with these issues since they are very delicate in nature.

Consideration 3

For some individuals, providing care to aging parents or other relatives can create unique life role demands. This is the **sandwich generation**; namely, individuals caught between the often conflicting demands of caring for children and elder family members. Women shoulder much of the childcare responsibility within two-parent households, even when both parents are in the labour force.[51]

This also holds true for elder care, both in terms of the likelihood of providing care and in performing the most intensive tasks such as bathing, dressing, and cooking.[52] For these mothers, working out a flexible work arrangement is often a necessity, which allows them to be better caregivers and employees.[53] As 35% of the sandwich generation has reportedly changed their work schedule to accommodate for these types of changes, it is an alternative that employers might want to explore with their employees, especially when a newborn is involved.[54]

Leading Practice Snapshot:

KPMG LLP is an accounting and professional services firm with over six thousand employees. They provide a number of benefits to new parents, including top-up payments (up to 100% of salary for seventeen weeks) as well as parental top-up for new fathers and adoptive parents. The company also offers adoptive parents a generous subsidy to help cover the costs of adoption (up to $20,000).

ADOPTIVE MOTHERS

Consideration 1

Currently in Canada, biological mothers are allotted fifteen weeks of maternity leave benefits to recuperate from the stress and physical hardships endured by pregnancy. In addition, they are given thirty-five weeks of employment insurance benefits (for use by either parent, or both). Adoptive parents are not given the fifteen weeks of maternity leave benefits that biological mothers receive. However, these parents must still deal with stress and costs associated with the adoption process, and they need to spend time to integrate their child into their new environment. Although this may not be an issue that can be resolved by the employer, it is important for employers to be aware of the stress that can be endured by adoptive parents. Intuitively, employers may not believe that adoptive parents have as many commitments both prior to and after the birth of their child. Far from these assumptions, adoptive parents often need to take off time prior to the arrival of their child for travel and various appointments.

Consideration 2

Adoptive mothers often deal with timeframes that are unpredictable. They can be unsure as to how long the adoption process will take, and an adoptive mother may need to tend to the birth mother at different points of her gestation period for a variety of reasons. The employer must meet this uncertainty with flexibility, and it is important for both parties to have an open line of communication, so no one is met with unwanted surprises.

"The goal of leave is the well-being of my child, and an adoptive child is at least as vulnerable and needy in terms of emotional support as a birth child." – Employee Quote

---

NEW IMMIGRANT MOTHERS

Consideration

Many new immigrant mothers (in Canada for less than five years) are less likely to be able to access paid maternity benefits. This often occurs because the criteria for receiving employment insurance are strict and/or the new immigrant mother is simply ineligible (i.e., she is a part-time or contract worker). So what can employers do to help these employees, given that they may not be eligible for financial support? One feasible alternative is to provide them with social support.

Immigrant mothers identified social support as a key factor in successfully navigating their maternity leave in Canada; however, they are the ones who report that they received less social support during their pregnancy compared to Canadian-born women. This leads to feelings of isolation and seclusion.[55] The social support systems of new immigrant families are often thousands of miles away and are not always accessible. In a study by Reitmanova and Gustafson, women often expressed a desire to have someone from their community with previous maternity experience to spend time with them.[56] Indeed, employers could offer both support in the form of mentorship programs, and provide new immigrant mothers with information about resources (e.g., household help, reassurance, and financial assistance), which they are less likely to receive simply due to lack of knowledge.[57]

ABORIGINAL MOTHERS

Consideration

Like new immigrant mothers, some aboriginal mothers will seek mentorship to guide them along cultural traditions other family and community members upheld during their pregnancy. That is, some aboriginal women may hold different pregnancy traditions and routines. Employe rs may need to give special consideration to this population when time and accommodations are needed for doctor's appointments.[58] Providing aboriginal women with an environment that is absent of stigma and judgment is imperative when they are practicing their traditional beliefs.

SAME-SEX MOTHERS

Consideration

In the workplace, same-sex parents can, for the most part, face similar concerns as heterosexual parents. They fear that their employers will view them as less productive, and this influences how much time they are likely to take for parental leave. When employers provide their employees with a socially supportive workplace, they will feel more comfortable with the length of time they choose to take for their maternal/parental leave.

In regards to length of parental leave, within a female same-sex relationship, the partner who carries the child will receive the fifteen weeks that are allotted to women to recover from the physical hardship of labour. In addition to this time, same-sex parents are given the same amount of time for parental leave. For some same-sex partnerships, adoption may be the only viable option when considering parenthood. In most provinces and territories, same-sex partners can adopt a child together. Much like adoptive parents, same-sex parents may have to travel to meet their child or surrogate. This may mean unpredictable timelines and schedules, and employers will have to be ready for their employee to leave at a moment's notice.

In this section we have outlined some important considerations that should be made when dealing with unique groups of women. This section was not meant to be exhaustive, and employers should be mindful that there are additional groups who also experience unique challenges while pregnant and parenting (e.g., parents who have multiple births, complicated pregnancies, and children with disabilities). However, one of the biggest steps an employer can take to help marginalized mothers feel more comfortable during and after pregnancy is to provide a socially supportive work climate that enables all individuals to gather the necessary resources and tools they need to maximize their leaves.

Fifteen Low/No Cost Employer Strategies
TO FACILITATE EMPLOYEE ENGAGEMENT

A quick review of the literature will tell you that employee engagement is positively correlated with employee productivity. But how does one facilitate employee engagement? Below you will find fifteen simple strategies to facilitate employee engagement and provide your organization with a competitive advantage. Employee engagement is undoubtedly good business, and the following strategies can help build it:

"There are a lot of things that would go a long way in supporting a new mom, that are not costly to the organization." - Employer Quote

---

1. **Relationships:** As an employer, it is important to know the job is getting done. But equally important, is knowing *who* is doing the job. Employers should invest the time and energy in getting to know their employees, and provide opportunities for employees to get to know one another (e.g., career background, current projects, education, special interests, and family composition). As an employer it is important to know your employees and understand their unique needs as working mothers. Good working relationships are key for collaboration, innovation, and adapting to change, such as maternity leave career transitions.

2. **Recognition:** Recognizing both employee effort and outcome can be a quick and easy way to show your appreciation. Recognition is also something that employees want more of from their employers, but

often do not know how to ask for it. Employee recognition should be timely and specific, noting exactly what was done well. It should also be unique to the individual; while one employee may appreciate an organization wide e-mail thanking her for her contributions, another may prefer a more discrete show of recognition. Small gestures such as verbal feedback, a gift certificate, or the privilege of leaving early to participate in her child's activity might just do the trick. When working mothers know that their effort and performance is appreciated and recognized, their level of commitment and accountability to the organization will also increase.

3. **Community:** Fostering a sense of community among employees is a great strategy to build trust, loyalty, and increase communication. Employees who feel valued and included are great ambassadors to organization stakeholders, including customers and future talent. Team building activities, such as a potluck lunches, lunch and learns put on by employees, or corporate volunteering initiatives, can foster a sense of unity and partnership. Some organizations have instituted initiatives to speak to the needs of various employees by creating parenting groups where employees can share information related to raising their children, and guest speakers are brought in to speak on a variety of parenting topics.

4. **Communication and transparency:** Sharing important organizational information in a timely fashion and having honest conversations will help employees understand how they fit into the organization's corporate strategy. Communicating information can also be a means of empowering a working mother to manage her career more effectively.

5. **Culture:** Create a workplace culture that is inclusive of and supports families. Celebrate different family compositions and consider having staff events where family members are welcome.

6. **Leadership:** It is imperative to lead by example. As such, leaders who are committed to family-friendly workplaces can motivate others in the organization to recognize the importance of well-managed maternity leave career transitions. Integrate your own work and home life to demonstrate to employees that integration is acceptable and fully supported.

7. **Facilitate:** Promote a culture that encourages development by facilitating opportunities for discussion and learning. While it is important to be aware of federal, provincial, or organizational policy regarding maternity leave, this transition has a significant impact on career development, making it essential to integrate the career development perspective into the discussion. Maternity leave can be equally and

uniquely impactful on women in senior and entry-level positions, so do not let a position title alone dictate the importance of the transition on the employee's career.

8. **Learning opportunities:** Employers are in a great position to provide learning opportunities and stretch assignments to working mothers. After facilitating a career dialogue, you will have more information about which tasks she is interested in and you will also be able to set the stage for development opportunities. Some working mothers report a loss of confidence in returning to work after a maternity leave, so when the timing is right, let her know that you have confidence in her knowledge, skills, and abilities, and want to further develop them through these opportunities.

9. **Autonomy:** Autonomy is a great strategy to promote accountability and increase the confidence of new mothers. Ensure that you have a discussion about what constitutes autonomy in order to set her up for success. To a working mother, autonomy may include *how* the task is completed, *when* she works, or *where* she gets the job done. Autonomy becomes increasingly important when a woman becomes a mother and is faced with the need to integrate her priorities and time.

10. **Success:** As an employer, do not assume an employee knows what is expected of her based on her job description. Goals must be clearly communicated. Defining clear goals and expectations, and providing employees with the necessary resources and support to achieve these targets sets employees, and you, up for success. Do not forget to take the time to understand what career success means to each working mother. Some may desire full-time positions with increasing pay and seniority, while others may prefer a part-time schedule or project-based opportunities. Using the same measuring stick to quantify success will disempower and disengage working mothers.

11. **Collaborate:** Taking the time to work together and gain the perspective of your employees is invaluable. Women report influencing approximately 64% of the household spending decisions, and so soliciting input from mothers in your workplace can provide you with a unique perspective or otherwise critical information needed for decision making and strategy.[59] Successful collaboration also allows you to communicate the reasoning behind changes to facilitate employee buy-in. Reaching out to an employee demonstrates that you are interested in hearing what she has to say.

12. **Develop:** Like other employees, working mothers wear many hats and have other interests independent of their family. Notice an employee's

interest/passion and explore the ways in which she can integrate or leverage that interest in the workplace, if possible, or encourage her to pursue it in her leisure time to support work-life integration. Employees will be motivated to engage in activities they are interested in and will report increased satisfaction with their employment when they engage in satisfying hobbies and leisure activities during their free time.

13. **Listen:** Avoid making assumptions about working mothers and ask questions instead. Many employers profess an open door policy, but this strategy is passive and puts the onus of initiating dialogue squarely on the employee. Be proactive, seek out and listen to input from working mothers. They may have unique ideas about how to improve efficiencies or better engage others.

14. **Mentor:** Encourage and facilitate mentoring opportunities within the organization. These mentorships can be based on technical expertise, life experience (e.g., successful maternity leave career transitions), or soft skills and attitude. A working mother may benefit from a mentor, but may be a great mentor, too. A well-matched mentoring relationship will benefit the mentor, protégée, and the organization.

15. **Coach:** As a busy employer, it can be easy to give an employee an answer to a specific concern or issue. Take a coaching perspective instead. Encourage the employee to explore the problem and pose solutions. "What do you think the major issues are and what do you think are some possible solutions we can explore?" Taking this approach will help develop her independence and confidence in her role.

Five Strategies with High Return on Investment

As discussed in the previous section, employers can invest in low/no-cost strategies to foster positive employee-organization relationships. In addition, organizations can commit (minimal) financial resources to roll out strategies with a high return on investment (ROI). Implementing any or all of these strategies will not only make employees feel cared for and supported by their organization, but it will also ensure that they are committed and efficient workers.

"If organizations just switched their approach and philosophy on maternity leave they would be able to reap the rewards." - Employer Quote

---

1. **Top-ups:** Of the employees who receive parental leave benefits, about one in five received **top-ups** by the organization.[60] This rate has remained stable for the past nine years, and organizations have, on average, supplemented their employees for less than six months.[61] One option for organizations to consider is to top-up their employees' wage from 90% to 100% of their salary for a portion of, or for the entire length of, their maternity leave. When high-potential candidates are seeking employment, these types of benefits can be a major attraction, thereby increasing the calibre of applicants and employees. According to a Statistics Canada survey, in 2008, within eighteen months of giving birth, 96% of women with paid benefits and a top-up returned to work

for the same employer, compared with 77% who had paid benefits and no top-up.[62]

2. **Time:** Employers can consider assigning family sick days, versus individual sick days, as a policy. Employers often do not let employees use their sick days for sick children, which is problematic given that when a child is sick, a parent is often needed to tend for the child, pick up the child from school, and take the child to appointments, among other responsibilities. If an employer does not formally allow their employees to take off at a moment's notice for these types of unforeseeable circumstances, employees might feel caught between a rock and a hard place or end up lying to the employer about why time off is needed. Ensuring that employees do not have to choose between these two responsibilities in times of sickness will result in a happier employee, which will, in turn, positively impact the organization's bottom line.

3. **Support:** In general, providing mentors for employees is important, and can be extremely helpful. However, it is equally important for an employer to be mentored by other employers who have effectively handled maternity leave transitions in the past. Most maternity leaves and policies focus on what employers can't do versus what they can and could be doing (shift approach to thou shall v. thou shall not). Seek organizations that have had prior success with maternity leave transitions, and conversely, share your stories if you have had success.

4. **Resources:** One common theme that is clear among new mothers is that they feel there is a lack of resources, and it is difficult to access the information they need. One consideration that mothers need to make when returning from maternity leave is finding childcare. Companies are in a position to develop relationships with reputable childcare providers (employees may have priority at certain daycares). By building these community bonds, organizations can develop employee family assistance plans to provide benefits like reduced childcare costs.

5. **Information:** In many instances, mothers-to-be argue that they are not even aware of the resources that are available to them within their community and their workplace. As a new mother, it can feel overwhelming to find a solution to a basic problem, and many struggle to know what questions to ask. Additionally, there is a lack of consistency in the information that is provided through a number of outlets, and it can be challenging to wade through. An employer can take responsibility and provide parents with the information they need to simplify their lives. By pooling collective resources, employers can provide parents

with clear and concise information on such things as parent networks, RESPs, and local family events/activities.

CONCLUSION

We hope you enjoyed reviewing this resource as much as our team has enjoyed putting it together. We also hope that you are able to acknowledge the successes you are having in supporting expectant and parenting women in your organization and are challenged to continually improve upon and integrate new and promising practices to *Make it Work!*

Glossary

Buddy system
Pairing women about to go on, or returning from, maternity leave with an employee who has already been through the maternity leave process and can offer advice and support through these transitions.

Career
The sum of all the paid and unpaid roles an individual has held in his or her lifetime.

Career development
The ongoing acquisition or refinement of knowledge, skills, and abilities.

Career dialogues
Future-focused conversations that highlight career opportunities for an employee both before and after returning from her maternity leave.

Career ladder
An concept that characterizes career progression as a vertical movement.

Career lattice
The notion that career progression can be characterized by movement in several directions, including: horizontal, vertical, downward, or diagonal.

Career progression
The movement towards a particular career goal(s). These goals are determined by the individual as important and worthwhile to pursue, and may or may not include a change in title, responsibility, status, pay, flexibility, influence, etc. (also referred to as 'career advancement').

Comeback coaching	Professional career transition support provided to a mother returning to work after a maternity leave or other extended leave. The coach may be an internal or external coach.
Employee	An individual within the organization whom you have the direct responsibility for managing.
Employee-centered strategies	Strategies that emphasize a collaborative and participatory approach between all parties with an organization, which support employees to become as effective as possible through company programs, processes, and policies. Employee-centered strategies recognize and place value on the unique talents and circumstances of each employee.
Employer	An individual who holds a leadership position within an organization and is responsible for overseeing staff members. For the purposes of this guidebook, employers can include, but are not limited to, managers, supervisors, executives, and business owners.
Exit interview	An interview conducted with an employee going on maternity leave, where the expectant mother provides feedback to improve aspects of the organization related to retention, reduced turnover, and employee development.
Expectant mothers	Mothers who, through birth or adoption, are expecting the arrival of a child.
Flexible hours	A schedule where an employee works a full day, but varies his or her hours, allowing flexibility at the start and end of the working day.
Flexible work arrangements	Alternative arrangements or schedules from the traditional working day and week.
Graduated return	Returning to one's regular work responsibilities after a leave, but with a gradual increase in time at work each day (or week) until the target hour is reached.
Groupthink	The practice of thinking or making decisions as a group in a way that discourages creativity and individual responsibility.

Inclusive workplace	A climate in which respect, equity, and positive recognition of differences are cultivated and leveraged.
Job-sharing	An alternative work schedule where two employees voluntarily share their responsibilities, salary, benefits, and time-commitments for one or more positions or sets of duties.
Marginalized mothers	Individuals who are excluded from some or all of mainstream social, economic, cultural, or political life. Marginalized mothers most affected by maternity leave may include young mothers, first time mothers over the age of forty, adoptive parents, aboriginal women, recently immigrated mothers, and same-sex mothers.
Maternity leave	The term inclusive of maternity, parental, and adoption leave, as well as any extended care and nurturing leave following the birth, or adoption of a child, taken by a new/expectant mother.
Maternity leave career transitions	Changes in the new/expectant mother's employment as a result of pregnancy, birth or adoption.
Mentorship	A developmental relationship where one individual with more knowledge and experience guides the lesser experienced individual.
Micro-affirmations	Subtle acknowledgments that recognize an individual's value and contributions.
Micro-inequities	Actions that stem from unconscious bias.
Motherhood penalty	The argument that working mothers in the workplace encounter systematic disadvantages in pay, perceived competence, and benefits relative to non-parents and men.
New-concept part-time employment	Positions that offer employees a higher income and more career opportunities than traditional part-time options, resulting in enhanced prestige and job satisfaction.
Part-time work	When an individual works less than thirty hours per week.
Postpartum depression	Depression experienced by a mother that may start during pregnancy or at any time up to a year after the birth of a child.

Professional development	Encompasses all types of facilitated learning and training opportunities associated with one's career and career progression.
Re-onboarding	The process of re-integrating an employee returning from maternity leave into the workplace. This can include training and introducing her to any changes that have occurred during her absence.
Return to work plan	A logistical plan created between an employer and an employee returning from a maternity leave, to help transition the new mother back to work.
Sandwich generation	Individuals who are responsible for the care of family members across two or more generations.
Soft return	An agreed upon start and end time where the employee may have a reduced or minimal workload the first few days or first week after her official return.
Sponsorship	A workplace relationship characterized by having an ally in the organization who has the power to effect change and actively advocates for career building opportunities.
Stakeholders	Any relevant third-party who has an interest in or is otherwise impacted by your business. This can include customers, clients, co-workers, and the community.
Telework	Working away from the traditional office space.
Top-ups	Income to supplement employment insurance benefits, which is offered to employees who are on leave, travelling, etc.
Unconscious bias	An assumption typically rooted in a stereotype or prejudice, which leads us to make misinformed and often inaccurate conclusions about a situation or another person.
Work-life integration	To create meaningful engagement between the interconnected roles, relationships, and responsibilities of an individual's life.
WORKshift	Working when and where an individual is most effective, which may include, but is not limited to, teleworking, flexible hours, and alternate scheduling.

Endnotes

1.   McQuillan, K. (2013). *All the Workers We Need: Debunking Canada's Labour-Shortage Fallacy*. SPP Research Paper, (6-16). Retrieved from: http://policyschool.ucalgary. ca/?q=content/all-workers-we-need-debunking-canadas-labour-shortage-fallacy

2.   Statistics Canada. (2014). *Canadian postsecondary enrolments and graduates, 2012/2013*. Retrieved from: http://www.statcan.gc.ca/daily-quotidien/141125/dq141125d-eng. htm.

3.   Statistics Canada. (2010). *Women in Canada: Paid Work, 1976-2009*. Retrieved from: http://www.statcan.gc.ca/daily-quotidien/101209/dq101209a-eng.htm.

4.   Statistics Canada. (2010). *Women in Canada: Paid Work, 1976-2009*. Retrieved from: http://www.statcan.gc.ca/daily-quotidien/101209/dq101209a-eng.htm.

5.   Statistics Canada. (2015). *International Women's Day...by the numbers*. Retrieved from http://www.statcan.gc.ca/dai-quo/smr08/2015/smr08_197_2015-eng.htm#a3)

      Statistics Canada. (2015). *Quarterly Demographic Estimates: April-June 2015*. Retrieved from: http://www.statcan.gc.ca/pub/91-002-x/91-002-x2015002-eng.pdf

6.   Canadian Human Rights Commission. (2014). *A Guide to Balancing Work and Caregiving Obligations: Collaborative approaches for a supportive and well-performing workplace.*

7.   Shipman, C., & Kay, K. (2009). Womenomics: Work less, achieve more, live better. New York: Harper Business.

8.   Joy, L., Carter, N., Wagner, H., & Narayana, S. (2007). *The Bottom Line: Corporate performance and women's representation on boards. Catalyst.*

9.   Joy, L., Carter, N., Wagner, H., & Narayana, S. (2007). *The Bottom Line: Corporate performance and women's representation on boards. Catalyst.*

10.   McKinsey & Company. (2010). *Women matter: Women at the top of corporations: Making it happen.*

        Shipman, C., & Kay, K. (2009). *Womenomics: Work less, achieve more, live better. New York: Harper Business.*

11.   Responsible Investment Association. (January 2015). *Canadian Responsible Investment Trends Report.* Retrieved from: http://riacanada.ca/wpcontent/uploads/2015/01/RI_Trends_Report2015_EN.pdf).

12.   Carr-Ruffino, N. (2005). *Making diversity work.* Upper Saddle River: Pearson Education Inc.

13.   Benko, C., Anderson, M., & Vickberg, S. (January 2011). *The Corporate Lattice: A strategic response to the changing world of work.* Deliotte University Press. Retrieved from: http://dupress.com/articles/the-corporate-lattice-rethinking-careers-in-the-changing-world-of-work/

14.   Williams, J., & Dempsey, R. (2014). *What works for women at work: Four patterns working women need to know.* New York University Press, New York.

15.   Bridges, W. (2003). *Managing Transitions: Making the Most of Change.* Da Capo Press, Cambridge MA.

16.   Kmec, J. A. (2011). *Are motherhood penalties and fatherhood bonuses warranted? Comparing pro-work behaviors and conditions of mothers, fathers, and non-parents.* Social Science Research, 40(2), 444-459.

17.   Kmec, J. A. (2011). *Are motherhood penalties and fatherhood bonuses warranted? Comparing pro-work behaviors and conditions of mothers, fathers, and non-parents.* Social Science Research, 40(2), 444-459.

18.   Kmec, J.A., Gorman, E. (2010). *Gender and discretionary work effort: evidence from the United States and Britain.* Work and Occupations, 37, 3-36.

19.   Marsden, P. V., Kalleberg, A. L., & Cook, C. R. (1993). *Gender differences in organizational commitment influences of work positions and family roles.* Work and Occupations, 20(3), 368-390.

20.   Wallace, J. E. (2008). *Parenthood and commitment to the legal profession: Are mothers less committed than fathers?* Journal of Family and Economic Issues, 29(3), 478-495.

21.   Meyer, J. P., Stanley, D. J., Herscovitch, L., & Topolnytsky, L. (2002). *Affective, continuance, and normative commitment to the organization: A meta-analysis of antecedents, correlates, and consequences.* Journal of Vocational Behavior, 61(1), 20-52.

22.   Barnett, R. C., & Hall, D. T. (2001). *How to use reduced hours to win the war for talent.* Organizational Dynamics, 29, 192-210.

23.   Kmec, J. A. (2011). *Are motherhood penalties and fatherhood bonuses warranted? Comparing pro-work behaviors and conditions of mothers, fathers, and non-parents.* Social Science Research, 40(2), 444-459.

24.   Heilman, M.E., Okimoto, T.G. (2008). *Motherhood: A Potential Source of Bias in Employment Decisions.* Journal of Applied Psychology, 93, 189–198.

25.   Kmec, J. A. (2011). *Are motherhood penalties and fatherhood bonuses warranted? Comparing pro-work behaviors and conditions of mothers, fathers, and non-parents.* Social Science Research, 40(2), 444-459.

26.   Carr, P.L., Ash, A.S., Friedman, R.H., Scaramucci, A., Barnett, R.C, Szalacha, L., Palepu, A., & Moskowitz, M.A. (1998). *Relation of Family Responsibilities and Gender to the Productivity and Career Satisfaction of Medical Faculty.* Ann Intern Med. 1998, 129(7), 532–538.

27.   Butterfield, Lalande, Borgen. (2008). *Canadian Research Working Group on Evidence Based Practice in career development.* Career Conversation Literature Review.

        London. (2005). *Career discussions at work: Practical tips for HR, managers, and employees.* Chartered Institute of Personnel Development.

28.   Kay, K., & Shipman, C. (2014). *The Confidence Code: The science and art of self-assurance-what women should know.* New York: Harper Business.

29.   Catalyst. (2011). *Fostering sponsorship success among high performers and leaders.* Retrieved from: http://www.catalyst.org/knowledge/fostering-sponsorship-success-among-high-performers-and-leaders

   Foust-Cummings, H., Dinolfo, S., & Kohler, J. (2011). *Sponsoring women to success. Catalyst.* Retrieved from: http://www.catalyst.org/publication/485/23/sponsoring-women-to-success

30.   Fudge, J. (2006). *Control Over Working Time and Work-Life Balance: A Detailed Analysis of the Canada Labour Code, Part III.* Human Resources and Skills Development Canada. Retrieved from: http://www.hrsdc.gc.ca/eng/labour/employment_standards/fls/pdf/research17.pdf

31.   Smith, B. (March2011). *What to expect when your employee's expecting. Benefits Canada Newsletter and Magazine.* Retrieved from: http://www.benefitscanada.com/benefits/health-wellness/what-to-expect-when-your-employee%E2%80%99s-expecting-14766

32.   WORKshift. (2015). *Environmental benefits of WORKshift.* Retrieved from: http://www.workshiftcanada.com/workshift-planet/benefits

33.   Blake, R. (2006). *Employee retention: What employee turnover really costs your company.* Retrieved from: http://www.iwaminstitute.com/assets/files/Articles/Employee%20Retention-What%20It%20Really%20Costs%20Your%20Company.pdf

34.   Friedman, D. E. (2001). *Employer supports for parents with young children.* The future of Children, 11, 62-77.

35.   WORKshift. (2015). *Environmental benefits of WORKshift.* Retrieved from: http://www.workshiftcanada.com/workshift-planet/benefits

36.   CCOHS. (2015). OSH answers fact sheets: *Telework/telecommuting.* Retrieved from: http://www.ccohs.ca/oshanswers/hsprograms/telework.html

37.   Statistics Canada. (2010). *Women in Canada: Paid Work, 1976-2009.* Retrieved from: http://www.statcan.gc.ca/daily-quotidien/101209/dq101209a-eng.htm.

38.   Williams, J.C., Manwell, J., & Bornstein, S. (2006). *"Opt Out" or Pushed Out? How the Press Covers Work/Family Conflict.* The Centre for Work-Life Law. Retrieved from: http://www.worklifelaw.org/pubs/OptOutPushedOut.pdfWorking Families. (2011). Discover

the benefits of job sharing. Retrieved from http://www.acas.org.uk/index.aspx?articleid=3568

39. Barnett, R. C., & Hall, D. T. (2001). *How to use reduced hours to win the war for talent.* Organizational Dynamics, 29, 192-210.

40. Kelly, E. L., Kossek, E. E., Hammer, L. B., Durham, M., Bray, J., Chermack, K., & Kaskubar, D. (2012). *Getting there from here: Research on the effects of work-family initiatives on work-family conflict and business outcomes.* Academy of Management Annals, 2, 305-349.

41. Lee, B. Y. L., & DeVoe, S. E. (2012). *Flextime and profitability.* Industrial Relations, 51, 298-316.

42. Wood, L. (November 2015). *Is job sharing the future? Workplace focus.* Retrieved from: http://www.workplacefocus.co.uk/ article/job-sharing-future

43. Katepoo, P. (2015). *Four compelling employer advantages of job sharing.* Retrieved from: http://www.workoptions.com/job-sharing-advantages

44. Gallo, A. (September 2013). *How to make a job sharing situation work. Harvard Business Review.* Retrieved from: https://hbr.org/2013/09/how-to-make-a-job-sharing-situation-work/

45. Lynk, M. (June 2008). *The Duty to Accommodate in the Canadian Workplace: Leading principles and recent cases.* Faculty of Law, University of Western Ontario, Ontario Federation of Labour. Retrieved from: http://ofl.ca/wp-content/uploads/2008.06.21-Report-DutytoAccommodate.pdf

46. Pulkingham, J., & Van Der Gaag, T. (2004). *Maternity/ Parental leave provisions in Canada.* Canadian Woman Studies, 23(3), 116-125.

47. Budak, J. (September 2011). *The dark side of maternity leave. Canadian Business.* Retrieved from: http://www.canadianbusiness.com/business-strategy/the-dark-side-of-maternity-leave/

48. Laughlin, L. (2011). *Maternity leave and employment patterns of first-time mothers: 1961 – 2008.* Household Economic Studies, 2-21.

49. Statistics Canada. (2014). *Canadian postsecondary enrolments and graduates, 2012/2013.* Retrieved from: http://www.statcan.gc.ca/daily-quotidien/141125/dq141125d-eng.htm.

50. Allen, V. M., Wilson, R. D., & Cheung, A. (2006). *Pregnancy outcomes after assisted reproductive technology.* Genetics Committee of the Society of Obstetricians and Gynaecologists of Canada; Reproductive Endocrinology Infertility Committee of the Society of Obstetricians and Gynaecologists of Canada. J Obstet Gynaecol Can, 28(3), 220-250.

Luke, B., & Brown, M. B. (2007). *Elevated risks of pregnancy complications and adverse outcomes with increasing maternal age.* Human Reproduction, 22(5), 1264-1272.

51. Silver, Cynthia. 2000. *Being there: The time dual-earner couples spend with their children. Canadian Social Trends* (Statistics Canada Publication No. 11-008-XPE) 57 (Summer): 26-29.

52. Ward, R., & Spitze, G. (1998). *Sandwiched marriages: The implications of child and parent relations for marital quality in midlife.* Social Forces, 77(2), 647-666.

Marks, N.F. (1998). *Does it hurt to care? Caregiving, work-family conflict and midlife well-being.* Journal of Marriage and the Family, 60(4), 951-966.

53. Williams, C. (2004). *The Sandwich Generation.* Statistics Canada Publication No. 75-001-XIE.

54. Williams, C. (2004). *The Sandwich Generation.* Statistics Canada Publication No. 75-001-XIE.

55. Kaczorowski, J., O'Brien, B., & Lily Lee, B. N. (2011). *Comparison of maternity experiences of Canadian-born and recent and non-recent immigrant women: findings from the Canadian Maternity Experiences Survey.* J Obstet Gynaecol Can, 33(11), 1105-1115.

56. Reitmanova, S., & Gustafson, D. L. (2008). *"They can't understand it": maternity health and care needs of immigrant Muslim women in St. John's, Newfoundland.* Maternal and Child Health Journal, 12(1), 101-111.

57. Sword, W., Watt, S., & Krueger, P. (2006). *Postpartum health, service needs, and access to care experiences of immigrant and Canadian-born women.* Journal of Obstetric, Gynecologic and Neonatal Nursing, 35(6), 717-727.

58. Hancock, H. (2006). *Aboriginal women's perinatal needs, experiences, and maternity services: A literature review to enable considerations to be made about quality indicators.* Ngaanyatjarra Health Service (ISBN: 978-0-646-47273-7).

59.   Silverstein, M., & Sayre, K. (2009). *Women Want More: How to Capture Your Share of the World's Largest, Fastest-Growing Market.* New York: Harper Business.

60.   Statistics Canada. (2010). *Employer Top-Ups.* Statistics Canada Publication No. 75-001-X.

61.   Statistics Canada. (2010). *Employer Top-Ups.* Statistics Canada Publication No. 75-001-X.

62.   Statistics Canada. (2010). *Classification of full-time and part-time work hours.* Retrieved from: http://www.statcan.gc.ca/eng/concepts/definitions/labour-class03b

      Statistics Canada. (2010). *Employer Top-Ups.* Retrieved from: http://www.statcan.gc.ca/pub/75-001-x/2010102/article/11120-eng.htm